The Bus Kids

The Bus Kids

Children's Experiences with
Voluntary Desegregation

IRA W. LIT

Yale University Press   New Haven and London

Set in Minion Roman by Integrated Publishing Solutions, Grand Rapids, Michigan.
Printed in the United States of America by Sheridan Books, Ann Arbor, Michigan.

Library of Congress Cataloging-in-Publication Data
Lit, Ira W.
The bus kids : children's experiences with voluntary desegregation / Ira W. Lit.
p. cm.
Includes bibliographical references and index.
ISBN 978–0–300–10579–7 (hardcover : alk. paper)
1. School integration—California—Case studies.
2. Kindergarten—California—Case studies.   3. Minorities—Education—California—Case studies. I. title.
LC214.22.C2L58 2009
379.2'63—dc22   2008021447

A catalogue record for this book is available from the British Library.

This paper meets the requirements of ANSI/NISO Z39.48-1992 (Permanence of Paper).

It contains 30 percent postconsumer waste (PCW) and is certified by the Forest Stewardship Council (FSC).

10   9   8   7   6   5   4   3   2   1

To Buddy for your inspiration;
To Elliot for your luminous mentorship;
and to my young friends in the Canford Program,
may your boldest aspirations be realized.

Contents

Acknowledgments

*The purpose of research is to get smarter about the
world in order to make it a better place.*

—Lee Shulman

This project is the result of a group effort. In my attempts to produce a piece of scholarship worthy in some small way of Lee Shulman's grand vision, I have relied heavily on the assistance, advice, motivation, insight, wisdom, graciousness, hospitality, and participation of numerous others. I have learned a great deal from this process, perhaps most notably that nothing of real value can be produced alone.

To the Canford students, your kindergarten classmates in the Arbor Town schools, and your Canford Program peers: You have been the true inspiration for this work in more ways than one. Your creative, enthusiastic, and undaunted approach to schooling and the world is vitalizing. I am grateful to have had the opportunity to explore your worlds with you. You have taught me more than I could have anticipated. I hope that through this work I have done justice to the valuable lessons you have allowed me to share with others.

To the Canford parents: Thank you for your openness to this project, your willingness to share your thoughts and opinions with a stranger, and, most important, your indulgence in allowing me to learn by observing and working with your children. Without your support and participation, educational researchers would have far fewer opportunities to peer into the lives of children, learn all they have to share with us, and, in turn, discover ways to improve upon the quality of their educational experiences.

To the Arbor Town teachers: I am grateful for the efforts of all of the teachers with whom I worked during this study, not only because of your efforts to sustain my work, but also because of the care, consideration, attention, and devotion you displayed toward your students, and the professional demeanor and seriousness with which you approached your work. I feel fortunate to be a part of a profession that can claim you as members.

To my colleagues and friends: To Rob Kunzman, Denise Pope, Alan Marcus, Debbie Faigenbaum, Karina Otoya Knapp, and Brad Joondeph. Your assiduous readings and judicious suggestions have vastly improved the quality of this final product. More important, your advocacy, friendship, and good humor were immensely sustaining throughout this process.

To my mentors: To Elliot Eisner, mentor and mensch. You epitomize the multiple roles of teacher, mentor, and sage, in a way that fulfills the promise of an apprenticeship better than I could have ever imagined. You have profoundly expanded my vision of and approach to the educational enterprise. To Ray McDermott, for asking the difficult questions and making me think harder and deeper about my work in critical and enduring ways. To John Baugh, for your years of support, encouragement, and respect in my multiple professional lives. And also to Buddy Peshkin, for helping me to plant those initial kernels and keeping watch over them for me. See how they've sprouted?

And to my family: To my parents, Judy and Jerome Lit, for instilling in me a love of children, education, and learning in the first instance, and for supporting me in the pursuit of those interests and ideals. To my in-laws, Jay and Julie Choo, for your advocacy and encouragement (and copious babysitting!), which have bolstered my efforts and family throughout this process. To my siblings, Amy, Terri, Lisa, Jeff, and Doug, for your interest in my work, affirmation of my dreams, and constant good humor which reminds me never to take myself too seriously. To Jim Gamble (and Terrie, Jamie, and Justin), for providing me with a home away from home and a place to grow up a second time around.

To Rachel Minjae, whose smile and delight make my world spin in ways I had never before dreamed possible; to Joseph Qyutae, for reminding me about what's truly important and for demanding that we tend to those things with regularity.

And, especially, to my wife, Jin, for encouraging me to follow this dream, for helping to create the structures and opportunities that provided for its (and my) nourishment along the way, for your patience and attentiveness when they were asked for, for your motivation and instigation when they were called for, and for helping to make this process one more rewarding adventure in our lifelong journey together.

Finally, a nod to my shortcomings: any errors, oversights, and omissions are all products of my own human limitations, and I take full responsibility for them.

I

Beginnings

In 1986, parties in a California school desegregation and racial discrimination lawsuit reached a settlement ending nearly ten years of rancor and litigation. The principal outcome of this agreement was the creation of a unique, voluntary, interdistrict transfer and desegregation program, later referred to as the Canford Program after one of the plaintiffs in the original lawsuit. In practice, the Canford Program provides opportunities for families of minority students from a racially segregated, under-resourced, and poor-performing school district to apply for a transfer to one of several surrounding elementary school districts, which are generally better resourced and better performing and serve primarily white students and families.[1]

The set of circumstances present in this program is particularly compelling. On the surface, at least, the Canford Program seems to provide a unique educational opportunity for a group of students who are traditionally counted among the at-risk or underserved. In certain ways, this opportunity boasts much of what educators have long argued for in the way of meeting the needs of all students. Students are afforded access to experienced, well-prepared teachers who are not overwhelmed by the circumstances of their vocation, and a strong, motivated peer group; teachers maintain high academic standards, are equipped with the necessary materials and support to teach toward them, and encounter low levels of bureaucratic oversight and interference.[2]

Given this special opportunity, how did the students fare in their crosstown schools? This book is the result of my efforts to explore the experience of students participating in the Canford Program, and to do so from the perspective of the youngest of those involved in the program. By spending two years in classrooms, on bus rides, and in the homes and after-school care settings of thirteen remarkable young children, I learned a great deal about the complex and dynamic enterprise undertaken by the Canford students. My hope is that in sharing and reflecting upon their compelling stories, I might help others to better understand the nature of this experience for the benefit of these students and others in similar situations.

The First Day of School: Two Perspectives

Shady Grove Elementary School sits high on a hill overlooking a quiet, suburban neighborhood in Arbor Town, California. The school building, consisting of three hexagonal wings extending from a central library, is reminiscent of a honeycomb. Each wing contains six classrooms divided by flexible, movable walls—a feature of 1970s-era "open classrooms" that now serves only as a historical relic. The classrooms all open both inward toward the central library and outward to an expansive outdoor play yard and capacious green fields. The effect of the school's architecture is a sense of fluidity reflected in the continuous, purposeful buzz of activity in and around the school throughout the day. Students and adults roam the vast corridors and entryways in a steady stream of movement and activity. When school is in session, this hive is alive!

It is early morning on a late August day. The sun shines brightly on the school and grounds. The air is tinged with excitement and anticipation as teachers, staff, and students begin to arrive for the first day of school.

The first youngsters to trickle in are older students—fourth and fifth graders who bike or walk to school on their own. They arrive early and eagerly begin getting reacquainted, building and reorganizing social ties and networks.

A bit later, other students begin to arrive with their parents. Some walk, some bike, and still others arrive by car. There is a great deal of chatter between, among, and across children and adults as they make their way to the school building and their respective classrooms. A wide variety of emotions can be read on the faces of both adults and children, though most seem excited and even joyful about the prospects of new beginnings.

Hand in hand, Megan and her mother, Sally, walk to Shady Grove Elementary. Though it is her first day of school at Shady Grove—Megan will be entering kindergarten today—she is quite familiar with the place. As they live nearby, Megan and her family have spent many hours at Shady Grove using the school's fields and playgrounds like a local park. In addition, Megan's older brother, Bill, is a third grader at Shady Grove; in fact, Megan's kindergarten teacher was also Bill's kindergarten teacher. Still, as Megan and Sally walk to the door of her classroom, Megan clings tightly to Sally, hiding most of her head and face behind her mother's shirtsleeve.

As they enter the classroom, Megan's teacher, Anita, immediately greets Megan and her mother. Anita has a gracious smile and a warm greeting for both Megan and Sally. Anita and Sally spend a few moments catching up as Anita helps Megan find and attach her nametag. Anita suggests that Megan take her mother to the cubbies and see if they can find the one assigned to her, and she points the pair in the appropriate direction. Then Anita hands Sally a flyer describing the numerous activity centers in the classroom. Anita proposes that after a quick "tour," Sally and Megan settle into an activity together until it is time for the class to gather at the meeting circle. "I'm so excited to have you in our class!" Anita says, as Megan and Sally set off on their tour and another family waits to be greeted and oriented.

Sally and Megan have arrived early, so the classroom is rather open and quiet. The activity centers are easily distinguished around the oddly shaped room: blocks in one corner, and building toys in another; a lofted playhouse overhanging a quiet reading space; three circular tables in the middle of the room, each replete with writing and drawing materials; and near the back door, a large circular rug bordered with the letters of the alphabet, hand-painted in gold and silver. Megan and Sally wind their way around the room, each in turn guiding the other, as they explore and get comfortable with Megan's new classroom.

Meanwhile, as the time nears for the first bell of the school day to ring, a traditional yellow school bus pulls up in front of the flagpole at the main entrance to Shady Grove. This bus, known as the Hills Bus, provides transportation for students within the large geographic area of the school attendance zone, particularly in the ranging hills to the north of the school site. As the students depart from the bus, a contingent of about a dozen adults are present, prepared to meet their youngsters riding the bus to school for the first time. The parents have taken the time to drive themselves to school while their children ride the bus, to greet them on the school side of the trip. In this way, parents are able to help facilitate their children's first-day transitions from home to bus to school to classroom. As they wait, the parents chat casually, outwardly excited and at ease with one another. Once the children arrive, they pair off with the adults, and parents engage children in conversations about the bus ride and their first day of school. The group then proceeds together toward the students' classrooms.

About five minutes later, at precisely 8:00 A.M., a digitized bell-tone sounds, signaling the official beginning of the school day and year. Several minutes later another bus arrives at the circular entryway to the school, which is now nearly deserted. This second bus is known as the SBC Bus. It transports interdistrict voluntary transfer students from South Bay City, a much less affluent city across the freeway, to various schools within Arbor Town. Because of the distance and the number of school sites involved, some of these students will have been in transit for nearly an hour by the time they reach their final destination.

This time two adults, both African American, are present to meet the school bus. The adults seem anxious and uncertain. As the bus begins to pull into the drive, one of the parents asks the other why no one from the school is there to greet the bus.

As the younger, mostly first-time students walk off of the bus, they congregate around these two adults. The parents ask the younger children about their bus ride while trying to elicit directions to classrooms from the older children. After a while, these parents wave down another adult (a classroom assistant at the school) who happens to be walking past the area. The two parents inquire why no one from the school has come to greet the bus and support the students. This assistant says she does not know, but she helps guide the parents and the children in the direction of their classrooms.

One of the new kindergarten students to arrive on the SBC Bus is named Marikit. Marikit's older sister, Michelle, is a second grader at Shady Grove. Michelle and Marikit begin to walk toward the school buildings with the small group of children who have congregated by the two adults. At some point Michelle runs off to her classroom, and the rest of the group wind their way around the building toward the primary classrooms. Eventually Marikit is dropped off in front of her room, and the rest of the group continue on to find their own.

As Marikit enters her new classroom—alone— her teacher, Anita, warmly greets her at the door. Anita assists Marikit in finding and placing her nametag on the front of her shirt. "Ooh! What a beautiful name you have! Did I say it right?" Anita asks. (She did not.) Marikit quietly repeats her own name as she glances around the busy room. Anita tries again to pronounce Marikit's name, and Marikit nods in approval. Anita then points Marikit in the direction of the cubbies and instructs her to put away her things and then choose an activity to work on before the first class meeting. From her perch at the doorway, Anita points out the drawing table, the reading area, and the playhouse in particular. Marikit turns toward the cubbies as Anita proceeds to welcome another late-arriving family.

As she moves toward the cubbies, Marikit is struck by an immense display of sights, sounds, people, and activities. By this time, the room is full of both children and adults, most of whom are busily engaged in activities. There is a cacophony of sounds as parents and children interact and engage one another in a multitude of ways. Marikit appears awestruck by the scene before her, but she proceeds to take her first cautious steps into her new classroom.

Marikit puts her things away in her cubby and slowly walks around the room. She looks somewhat apprehensively at many of the different activity centers. After a short time she stands near a table where children, most of whom are accompanied by a parent, are drawing with crayons. Marikit silently observes the other children working at the table. Soon thereafter, Anita comes by and asks Marikit if she would like to join the activity. Marikit nods in assent, and Anita helps to seat her in a chair and provides her with a piece of white paper and a set of crayons. Marikit holds a crayon and looks pensively at it and the paper. Moments later, just as Marikit begins drawing on her paper, Anita rings a small brass bell and sings out "Gather 'round, now! Gather 'round!" signaling that the time has come for the first "class meeting." Anita begins to gather the students together in a circle on the alphabet rug. As she does so, Anita walks over to Marikit and leads her toward the group by placing her arm around Marikit's shoulder and walking with her to the rug, where the two sit side by side. As Anita begins to greet the students, Marikit leans in toward Anita and nestles in under her arm.

Marikit and Megan are similar in many ways. They are both beginning their first day of kindergarten at Shady Grove Elementary. They both have siblings in the school and have been to the site on previous occasions, though Megan, who lives in the neighborhood, has done so with much greater frequency. Megan and Marikit are both five years old. Both of them are eager to begin school, and they both have some trepidation about the situation as well.

In many ways, of course, the two girls are also quite different. To the degree that individuals can be reflective of a larger group, Megan is a typical neighborhood student at Shady Grove.[3] Her family owns a home a short walk away from the school. Her father is a legal librarian at the law school in the neighboring university. Megan's mother is a marketing vice president in a large software company in Arbor Town. Megan is of mixed ethnic origin: her father is Jewish and her mother is Japanese. Both of her parents have graduate degrees and place a high value on education for their children.

Marikit, in her turn, is a typical student in the Canford Program in many ways. Her family rents a small home in South Bay City. Marikit's family is of Filipino origin, and English is not the family's primary language at home; however, Marikit has a strong capacity for comprehension and speaking in English. (This fact is difficult to discern initially, as Marikit is nearly silent for the first several weeks of school.) While both of her parents work—Marikit's mother is a nursing assistant and Marikit's father is a short-order cook—they still struggle to keep up in a geographic region where they are considered to be among the working poor. Marikit's mother has her GED and is taking night courses to earn a nursing degree. Her father completed two years of high school. Both of her parents place a high value on education for their children.

This narrative highlights some of the common elements in the experiences of Canford students attending schools in Arbor Town. Most of them arrive at school—often late—after an early morning wakening and a lengthy, difficult bus ride. Few Canford students have the benefit of a comforting parent to support the early morning transition to school, though they all have parents interested in their educational endeavors, evidenced at a minimum by their persistence and involvement in securing a rare slot in the program for their children. Once they arrive at school, the Canford students have access to the plentiful resources (materials, facilities, and personnel) of a school district with a strong reputation and high ratings on common measures of school achievement. At the same time, access to these resources requires the navigation of a complex series of challenges for participating students.

Canford parents have high hopes and expectations for the educational opportunities provided through this transfer program—and these dreams may well be warranted given the resources and general performance of the Arbor Town schools. Yet broadly speaking, few of the organizing participants involved (parents, teachers, or administrators) seem to take full account of the complexity of this endeavor for the program's children, nor do they seem to account for the potential impact of these challenges on the students' school experience. Underscored by Marikit's story and the others that follow, I believe, is the intricate nature of the Canford students' journey. I hope that through this book the reader can begin to see the layers of complexity that define the school experience for Marikit and other Canford students, as well as the ways this experience affects the lives of these young children.

Charting a Course

For six years before commencing my graduate studies, I taught kindergarten, third grade, and fifth grade in a public school district in northern California, one of the ten districts originally participating in the Canford Voluntary Transfer Program.

During that time I came to know an increasing amount about the Canford Program, though my knowledge was initially limited to personal experiences and interactions with students, parents, other teachers, and a select few administrators; the school and district provided no comprehensive orientation, information, or guidance regarding the program or its students. My personal educational philosophy manifests a strong belief in the value of social, cultural, and educational integration, as well as a conviction about the need for greater equity in educational opportunities and outcomes. Frequently, I wondered if and how these goals were being attended to or fostered through the Canford Program. What might be the benefits and drawbacks of the program for participating students and their school peers? What was the experience like for young children who left their own neighborhood to pursue educational opportunities in a distant community? Was opening the doors into such a setting enough to foster their success? Did we (teachers, administrators, and parents) know or do enough to support these students, who in many ways seemed to struggle in this environment? Over time, I became increasingly attracted to and interested in the experiences of the Canford students and their families. When I later determined to pursue a doctoral degree in education, my encounters with the Canford Program remained at the forefront of my mind, and thus the seeds of this book were sown.

My early exploration of the Canford Program revealed an intriguing history and distinct possibilities for further study. Sixteen years after its inception, 2,219 students had accepted transfers as part of the program, and yet virtually no effort had been undertaken during that time to explore the experiences or perspectives of participants, families, educators, and community members affected by the program, or the outcomes and impact of the program itself. Such a bold experiment demanded further examination.

As I began to consider the design of a research project, many promising avenues of pursuit seemed to be open, since so little work had been undertaken in regard to the program. By both necessity and interest, though, I narrowed my focus to a particular piece of this terrain. In general terms, this book is designed as a qualitative exploration of the experience of kindergarten students in their first year as participants in the Canford Program. My goal was to learn about the broad range of experiences relevant to this important transitional year and to illuminate the quality of life in schools for these young children. Domains of interest included the social, emotional, cultural, and developmental as well as the academic. General questions that helped to guide my study included the following: What was the experience like for the Canford students? What were their daily routines? How well did these students adjust to and fit into a geographically distant neighborhood school setting? What kinds of social connections did they make? How did they interact with peers and teachers? What opportunities and hurdles did they encounter? How did they feel about their experiences? What seemed to support and what seemed to impede their development? Broadly, what did these young children have to teach us about their experience that could be applied to other similarly situated students?

I believe that the Canford Program is illustrative as well as unique, and it deserves attention on both counts. The program is unique in its inception and design: ten school districts entered into a voluntary agreement to enhance the educational opportunities primarily for students in one of those districts, and they did so by providing enrollment opportunities for interested parents. At the same time, this program illustrates a host of educational phenomena of potential interest. For example, discussions about school choice programs, from magnet and charter schools to voucher programs, currently abound in the policy arena. The federal No Child Left Behind Act explicitly provides for school transfers as one means of redressing the ongoing failure of schools to meet national standards. The experience of the Canford students may well have something to teach us about such plans and programs. Embedded in the day-to-day lives of the Canford students are other issues of substance, including school desegregation and integration; busing; the processes of school transition, socialization, and adaptation; heterogeneity of classrooms and schools; the efforts of schools and teachers to support diverse student populations; issues of race, language, and culture; and questions of educational equity, to name just a few. Too rarely in our local and national debates do we reflect on the nature of the experiences we are creating from the point of view of the children involved. The experiences of the Canford students may shed light on larger issues, drawing our attention both to the day-to-day experience of the children involved and to the larger issues entwined in it. Ideally, such investigations will enhance our ability to make decisions and successfully implement the complex policies that have real-world consequences for children.

I think it is important to be clear about the aims and limits of this work from the outset. First, I want to clarify for the reader that this is not an evaluative study. It does not measure the program's overall "success," or critique the choices of parents who enroll their children in this and other such programs, or provide a cost-benefit analysis of the tradeoffs entailed in participation, though each of these aims is valuable in its own right. Rather, this book was designed as a qualitative

exploration of the lived experiences of the youngest participants in this novel program aimed at providing opportunities
for educational achievement and social integration.[4]

My primary purpose is to illuminate the unique qualities
and character of the life of these students. To that end, I have
produced a narrative study. The work contains observations,
descriptions, vignettes, quotations, dialogue, and my own perspectives and analyses. This approach borrows from a rich tra-
dition in the qualitative or ethnographic mode, including the
works of Alan Peshkin, Philip Jackson, and Vivian Paley, to
name just a few. My primary research tool was my work as a
participant observer in the schools and classrooms of thirteen
kindergarten students over the course of two academic years.
In addition, I spent time with students on the bus, in their
after-school programs, and in their homes. I interviewed parents, teachers, and administrators, and I also used a variety of
interview formats to elicit the perspectives of the students in
this study. Each of these approaches enhanced my understanding of the educational endeavors of the Canford students. (See the appendix for further discussion of research
methods.)

This work is organized with an eye toward illuminating
the experience of the *students* in this program, taking account
of and valuing their own perspective and experience. Far too
little research in education emphasizes the student point of
view, and this is particularly true for the youngest of our grade
school students. In the words of Philip Jackson in *Life in Classrooms* (1990), "We had better move up closer to the immediate
experience of young children if we are to discover what life in
the classroom is really like. In short, we had better get to our
informants while the smudge of chalk dust is still on their
sleeves."

At its core, my research is about the experience of a group of minority students whose parents take advantage of an opportunity to transfer their children out of an impoverished and poor-performing school district and into a neighboring district with a predominantly white student population that is affluent and high performing. An illustration of this set of circumstances may well have implications for many young children and educators, both those in this program and also those in similar settings.

My aim, then, is to elucidate for the reader some of the texture and depth of the Canford students' experiences. If successful, this effort will focus some attention on spaces and places in the educational lives of young children that we often overlook, ignore, or believe to be either irrelevant to or beyond the scope of our work as educators. I am hopeful that we might expand our understanding of the possibilities of schooling and education and think more deeply about how our roles as educators might encompass the needs of our students, their families, and their communities.

II
The Canford Program

Before moving into an exploration of the experience of students participating in the Canford Program, we shall first delve, at least briefly, into the history and background of this unusual educational experiment. What were the circumstances that led to this particular struggle for school integration and educational equality? What conditions and forces prevailed in the creation of such a unique, multidistrict resolution to these complex problems? What follows is a brief historical account addressing those questions.[1]

The 1954 Supreme Court decision in *Brown v. Board of Education* is typically referred to as the watershed moment in the struggle for school desegregation. Yet *Brown*, of course, did not immediately or effectively lead to the direct integration of our nation's public schools. In fact, by 1967 more than 80 percent of African American children in the South still attended segregated elementary and secondary schools.[2]

The Canford story begins in earnest in the mid-1970s, a time of significant developments in our national struggle to achieve the promise of *Brown*. Two Supreme Court cases in the early 1970s, *Green v. County School Board* (1968) and *Swann v. Charlotte-Mecklenburg* (1971), affirmed the Court's view that *Brown* required school districts to actively remove the vestiges of public-sanctioned discrimination, through such remedies as mandatory busing and gerrymandering attendance zones to achieve racial balance in public schools.[3] These cases led to sweeping changes in school assignment policies in numerous school districts across the country, with a concurrent wave of social and political upheaval. It is important to remember that California and other western states, while removed in large part from the turmoil in southern states and northeastern cities, were also grappling with complex issues of educational equity and integration in a variety of ways; most major metropolitan areas in the West, including Los Angeles, San Francisco, Denver, and Seattle, had desegregation programs of one kind or another at some point. And, important for our purposes, parents, educators, and the courts involved in the Canford story were all affected by the tenor of this historical period.

Geographic and Racial Isolation in South Bay City: The Development of a Segregated City and School District

For much of its history, South Bay City was an unincorporated township under the purview of the local county. The area is bounded by a waterway to the east and a freeway to the west. By the 1960s South Bay City had evolved into an almost entirely African American community, geographically isolated, racially segregated, and economically disadvantaged compared to all of its municipal neighbors. Children in South Bay City attended local elementary schools in the South Bay City Elementary School District. Mirroring the local population's demographics, by the end of the 1960s minority students, primarily African Americans, composed 90 percent of the South Bay City school population. Resources of South Bay City schools were meager compared with neighboring districts, as the city had a weak tax base from which to fund local schools. Additionally— perhaps as a result—South Bay City schools did not fare well on state and national exams, ranking among the lowest performers in the state of California. Meanwhile, South Bay City's district neighbors ranked among the most successful on both state and national exams.[4]

Upon completing the eighth grade, students from South Bay City and seven neighboring elementary school districts moved to one of several schools in the Redwood Regional High School District. The district faced two principal issues as students from South Bay City's struggling schools matriculated into the local high schools.

The majority of South Bay City students attended Dunnmeyer High, located within the geographic boundaries of the South Bay City Elementary School District. From 1958 to 1969, Dunnmeyer became an increasingly segregated school; its proportion of African American students increased from 21 percent to more than 90 percent as the demographics of South Bay City rapidly shifted. During this time, parents in neighboring communities whose children were assigned to Dunnmeyer fought battles with the district over school boundary lines, increasingly applied for transfers to one of the other district high schools, and moved out of the school boundary zone to avoid placement at Dunnmeyer. As Dunnmeyer became increasingly segregated, academic opportunities and external measures of school achievement also declined. Dunnmeyer's reputation suffered with district parents, and the cycle of segregation and underachievement worsened.

While the issue of school *segregation* was looming at Dunnmeyer, the district was also struggling with issues of the effective *integration* of its student body in neighboring high schools. The school district attempted to ameliorate the enrollment situation at Dunnmeyer by offering greater opportunities for student transfers, which would increase integration at all of the high schools. While very few students opted to transfer into Dunnmeyer, the minority enrollment in a few of the other district high schools began to rise as students from Dunnmeyer transferred to the more successful schools within the district. In the late 1960s, Valley High, with a minority population of about 15 percent, became the site of significant racial tension. The school and district were not prepared to cope with the differing needs of students from widely divergent racial and cultural backgrounds. Several race-related conflicts erupted on campus, eventually galvanizing the community. One campus incident in the fall of 1967, requiring the assistance of several local police officers and described as a near riot in local papers, seemed to provide a catalyst for parental and community action.

With heightened national attention to the issues of school desegregation, busing, and educational equality serving as a backdrop, the situation in the district's high schools garnered a great deal of scrutiny from state and federal officials, the school board, concerned parents, and community members. In turn, the Redwood Regional High School District and community members made several unsuccessful attempts to ameliorate the situation of growing disparity, segregation, and racial tension in its high schools. These efforts included attempts at increasing school integration through voluntary transfers and boundary extensions; a voluntary busing program; the implementation of a magnet program at Dunn-

meyer; the creation of several community and parent organi-
zations focused on the issues of segregation, integration, and
educational equity and opportunity; and an attempt to for-
mulate a ballot initiative to integrate schools across district
boundaries.[5]

Taking the Case to Court

As it became more evident that these complex issues were not
going to be resolved through either local policy-making or
community-based organizing, several individuals began making
the legal case for increased integration in the local schools. The
principal lawsuit was filed by a group of thirty-four parents
(both minority and nonminority) seeking an interdistrict, multi-
county solution to their concerns. The suit named as defen-
dants the State of California, the State Board of Education, two
county school superintendents, and ten school districts. The
claimants suggested that students in all districts named in the
suit were victims of an inadequate education, based on the segregation of regional schools. The suit was filed in a California
state superior court in June of 1976.[6]

The court proceedings were long and rocky, with head-
way and setbacks for the claimants over nearly a decade. The
issues were complicated by an evolving understanding of the
legal issues at hand in both the state and federal courts. A
major turning point in the case occurred in 1983, when a California appellate court acknowledged the existence of de facto
segregation among the school districts. Although the court
imposed limits on some potential remedies, such as mandatory
busing and pupil assignment, it declared that "all other desegregation techniques may still be utilized by the court to allevi-
ate de facto segregation."[7] This ruling set the stage for invigor-

ated settlement talks, though it took the parties another three years before a final settlement was signed, in March of 1986. As stated in the papers filed with the Superior Court, the major goals of the settlement were as follows:

> To the extent reasonable and feasible, to further equal opportunities for all students in all respondent districts by
> (1) reducing minority racial isolation among or between the students of the respondent districts' elementary schools,
> (2) improving the educational achievement in South Bay City schools, and
> (3) enhancing inter-district cooperative efforts.[8]

The most significant long-term outcome of the settlement agreement has been the implementation of the Canford Voluntary Transfer Program. Through this program, parents in the districts covered by the Canford agreement may apply for a transfer either into or out of the South Bay City School District. In practice this stipulation has meant the availability of a fixed number of slots in each of the surrounding districts for students from South Bay City.[9]

Participation in the program is voluntary and limited to the number of available spaces each year. Families of all incoming kindergarten students in South Bay City are notified of the program by the county office of education via a form letter. Interested parents apply to the county, which helps to administer the program. Parents can rank preferences for districts but not for schools. Districts assign students to schools as they deem appropriate. Overall, the program has been greatly sought after by South Bay City parents, and in the districts closest to South Bay City, particularly Arbor Town, there are waiting lists for admittance to the program each year.[10]

The Canford Program in Arbor Town

Since 1987, the Arbor Town School District has made approximately sixty slots available to transfer students each year, nearly all of whom enter the program (by design) in kindergarten. Over the first sixteen years of the program a total of 2,219 students accepted transfers as part of the Canford Voluntary Transfer Program, and 1,112 of them transferred to the Arbor Town School District.[11] In 1997 the program's first cohort of students graduated from Arbor Town high schools. During this time period, the attrition rate of participants from Arbor Town was approximately 40 percent, and most of those left the program when their families moved from the area. About 12 percent of transfer students left Arbor Town and returned to South Bay City schools, but little is reported about the factors leading to their choice.[12]

Through its own limited internal studies, Arbor Town has determined that the Canford Program has had a positive effect on participating students, although in interviews, district administrators acknowledge the difficulty of making this judgment. Internal reviews (which are infrequent) have been based primarily on student grades, attrition rates, parent surveys, and a limited analysis of standardized test measures. For example, school district officials have compared standardized test scores of Canford students in Arbor Town with those of students in South Bay City as a whole, finding that on average, Canford students score significantly higher than their peers in South Bay City schools but significantly lower than their peers in Arbor Town.[13]

While consideration of the academic progress of these students is certainly both relevant and important, it is also clearly not representative of the entire experience of these students and thus inadequate in forming an overall picture of the program. The social and emotional state of the students, their capacity to make and foster friendships, their comfort level and interactions with teachers and other school staff members, their level of acceptance and comfort in the school environment, the various roles they play in these settings, and many more telling signs of the richness of the students' experiences should also be tapped. My hope is to build upon the limited knowledge of this program by examining the experience of its youngest participants over the course of their kindergarten year as transfer students in the Arbor Town school district.

III
The Bus Kids

The Wheels on the Bus

I arrive at the bus yard at 6:20 A.M. It's early and I am tired. The day is cold, gray, and dreary. A light mist hovers over the vast asphalt parking lot, which is surrounded by a tall chain-link fence. Inside the gate are a few portable buildings and about two dozen traditional yellow school buses, several of which have their engines running. Diesel fumes infuse the air. My visual, auditory, and olfactory senses all provide strong confirming evidence that I have found the right place.

After checking in with the lead dispatcher, I exchange pleasantries with my bus driver, and we head toward our chariot, the "B" Bus, so noted by a plastic placard in its front window.

"So. You're pretty brave, huh?" the driver says to me with a smile. "They get a little wild, but they're pretty good kids. Hope you enjoy the trip." And with that we walk up the rubber-matted steps and onto the bus.

Once inside, the scene is quite familiar. I note the thirteen empty rows of high-backed benches covered in dark green vinyl. There is room enough for two children on each bench, three with a squeeze. (Filled to maximum capacity the bus can hold seventy-eight children, three to a bench.) I walk about six rows down the aisle and take a seat to the right of the driver, hoping to provide some distance between me and the only (other?) authority figure present once the children climb aboard. The air is chilly, and when I take my seat I can feel the cold, smooth vinyl cushion and the hard metal frame of the bench underneath my legs. A shiver runs through my body, and I draw my arms in tight around my chest. The driver closes the squeaky pneumatic doors, and we begin to bump slowly across the as-phalt and toward the city streets. Eventually we wind our way from Arbor Town across the freeway to South Bay City, about a three-mile drive. As we make a sharp stop at a traffic light I pitch forward in my seat, and I note that there are no seat belts on the bus, except for the driver's.

At 6:55 A.M. we pull up to our first stop and five students board the bus. They appear to be first or second graders, and they walk quietly onto the bus and take a seat in the first few rows. I am still shivering, but I note that two of the students are wearing short sleeves.

In all, the bus makes thirteen stops in South
Bay City before we begin to head back across the
freeway toward our Arbor Town school destina-
tions. The trip has taken us thirty-five minutes to
this point, and there are now approximately fifty
children on the bus (kindergarten through fifth
grade), with many students crammed three to a
bench. Generally, the older students are sitting in
the back of the bus and the younger ones are up
front, nearer the bus driver. The scene is chaotic.
Students are yelling, laughing, chatting, singing,
and crying throughout the bus. The noise level is
deafening, making it difficult to understand conversations with children even in the rows nearest to
mine. As I look around, I notice that there are only
two Anglos on the bus, the bus driver and myself.
The students are a diverse group, a reflection of the
desegregation goals of the Canford Program.

The activities on the bus cover a wide range.
Three girls near me are engaged in a song and
hand-clapping activity in Spanish. Two boys, one
sitting on a bench behind the other, are playing a
form of tag: one leans over the bench and slaps the
other on the head, then the second boy reaches
around the side of the bench and tries to give a slap
back. At one point, one of the boys is hiding underneath the seat. Another young boy sitting next
to me climbed aboard the bus with tears running
down his cheeks. As he made his way down the
aisle with his jacket hood half-covering his face, I
intercepted him to see if I might be of assistance.
He has yet to speak to me, but he seems to have

stopped crying and is resting his head against my arm.

The activity in the back of the bus is even more vigorous than it is near the front. Given how boisterous things are in the back, perhaps the younger students prefer the relative security of being near the bus driver. The older boys, in particular, are rowdy and loud. Several of them build a checkpoint of sorts by leaning their bodies into the aisle, about three-quarters of the way to the back of the bus. These boys harass other students and make it difficult for them to pass into the last few rows of benches. The driver seems to tacitly acknowledge their authority over the back benches by reserving seats for the younger students near the front.

Several students are out of their seats, especially in the back of the bus, either sliding across the aisleway toward another bench or leaning over and around the benches to talk or otherwise engage with other students.

From time to time, I hear the bus driver holler from her perch in the front of the bus as she peers into the rear view mirror. "Boys!" she calls out loudly at one point. Several children look up, and they can see her reflection in the oversized rearview mirror.

"I don't want to see any hitting, Antonio!" she yells.

"He say 'coconut head' to me!" one of the boys near me calls back.

"I don't want to see any hitting!" she says again, more slowly this time, then turns her attention back to the traffic.

The remainder of our ride proceeds in much the same fashion. When we finally pull up to the school at 7:55, the first students on the bus have been riding for about an hour, the last aboard for about twenty-five minutes. Personally, I feel a sense of relief, a lifting of a strong sense of anxiety, as I follow the last student down the steps of the bus and onto the school grounds. I briefly think back to my own days as a teacher and reflect on how I would greet my students in the morning as they walked into my classroom, hoping that we might begin the school day on a positive note. Clearly for these students their "school day" is already well under way!

Like many other transfer and desegregation plans, the Canford Program relies on busing as the primary means of transporting children from South Bay City to their Arbor Town schools. The Canford students' experiences on the bus play a significant role in their lives. Why is this transitional event so important? Perhaps precisely because the experience for the Canford students *is* one of transitions: the transition to primary school; the transition from one city and one neighborhood to another; for many, the transition from a native to a second language; and the transition from one set of cultural, community, and institutional norms to another. Hence, the bus plays a role in providing the means and perhaps also the occasion for the students to facilitate these myriad transitions. Moreover, the bus ride serves as label as well as allegory for Canford students: though not all Canford students ride the bus, as a group they are often referred to as the Bus Kids by district teachers.

Additionally, from a purely logistical standpoint, many Canford students spend a large part of their school day on the bus. Some students spend nearly two hours on the bus rides to and from school. For students on a half-day kindergarten schedule, that's over half as much time as they are actually at the school site (about three and a half hours per day). Even with a full six-hour day, some students spend about 25 percent of their school day on a bus.[1] Clearly the bus ride is a significant feature of the school experience for these students.

I pursued this particular topic over the course of my study by attending to the locations of the transitions to and from the bus; by asking related questions of teachers, students, and parents; and, perhaps most significantly, by spending time riding the bus with students. The preceding description of a typical ride on the school bus serves as a window into the Canford students' schooling experiences more generally. The enterprise is complex and difficult, making an already rigorous process of adjustment and adaptation to school even more challenging. It also acts as one of the many forces that tend to push the Canford students to the periphery of activity in the Arbor Town school setting, underscoring their status as outsiders. In this chapter, I take a look at some of the issues that are highlighted by this crosstown bus trip.[2]

How does the bus trip affect the start of the day for Canford students? Anita, one of the Arbor Town kindergarten teachers I worked with, described it this way: "Probably the biggest difference that I see [between the neighborhood students and the Canford students] is maybe what happened in the morning is so much different—before the kids get here. The 'Bus Kids' just come jangled. Sometimes they come hungry, because they have to get up so early to get the bus. They come upset. And that's, you know, that's the only thing about these, these two Canford girls, because they're so . . . their skills are so high. They're so bright. It's more . . . what happens on the bus. What happens before they get to school. I'm thinking for *these* kids it makes a difference . . . and I don't know how to deal with that."

The school day at Shady Grove Elementary school begins at 8:00 A.M. Teachers, students, and parents are often heard complaining about the early start, and certainly many individuals in each category arrive weary and lethargic at times. Students who ride the bus to school are generally expected to meet the bus between 6:55 and 7:30, depending on their stop. Between the early wakening and the potentially long and disorderly bus ride, students often arrive at school tired, cranky, hungry, and "jangled."

Delia, another kindergarten teacher, echoes Anita's concerns: "So, the bus ride really rushes them, and they're hungry by the time they get here and then it's so different. I just think the whole thing; I wish it could be easier for them. Because I think just being here is a big change."

Another teacher, Allison, notes that the bus ride would sometimes leave one of her students "hyped up for the whole day, just having that, because I'm sure . . . I think his home . . . I think is very tranquil and peaceful. Um . . . but the bus would just, you know, jack him right up."

Given the nature of the bus ride, perhaps it is not surprising that these young students encounter difficulties with their adventures on the bus. In the segments that follow, I elaborate more specifically on some of the consequences of the bus ride on the lives of the Canford students.

The Driver on the Bus Says, "No Hitting!"

The practicalities of the bus ride are only part of the story. The bus is often a place of conflict and concern for the Canford students, who experience physical confrontations, verbal disagreements, mocking and abusive taunts, and a sense of general dismay over the bus ride. The following are just a few examples of the upheaval that arises from the bus ride.

Pam, an Arbor Town teacher, notes the general sense of discord that is established on the bus and its impact on the students in the school setting: "A lot of times, riding the bus is an issue. Fights and disagreements occur on the bus ride that are carried into the classroom and onto the playground, and that's what happened a few years ago. I had three Canford kids. They all rode the bus. I had two boys and one girl and they were at odds the whole time. They got off the bus fighting. They fought all year together, but yet they stayed together. They never entered into any other social group at all."

Tali, a Canford student, talks about some of the abuse she receives at the hands of older students on the bus. When asked if she likes to ride the bus, Tali shakes her head from side to side, indicating "no." I ask why.

Tali replies, "One time when I rided on the bus a big kid spit on my face."

I ask what she did about it, and Tali says she told her mom. Later she says, "Today the big kid said they'll spit on me again if I don't sit by my own seat."

Numerous other examples of abusive language and insults emerge. For example, I ask another Canford student, Hector, if he likes riding the bus:

"Nope," Hector replies.

"Why not?" I ask.

"'Cause," Hector says.

"'Cause why?" I ask.

"'Cause people say 'cheesseey-head' and stuff to me."

"And you don't like that?" I ask.

"A little bit. And sometimes they put me to another spot, and I don't like that too." Another student, Felix, adds, "They say bad words there." In addition, some of the older boys taunt

Felix as he makes his way to his seat: "Ooh, boy!" the boys point and laugh at Felix. "You got big ears! Big ears!"

These interactions may appear to be the typical behavior of schoolchildren or, perhaps, a modest set of disagreeable tradeoffs in the pursuit of larger and more important aims. While there may be some truth to both of these claims, it is crucial to remember that these children are engaged in a compulsory activity, organized by the educational system yet buttressed by minimal supervision or other supports. The five- and six-year-old students have little, if any, comprehension of the larger issues at stake, and they have few of the skills necessary to negotiate these various challenges. The big question evident here for educators is where their responsibility begins and ends for the children in their care. If the bus ride is an experience organized in support of our educational aims, do we not have a responsibility to consider the educational impact of that experience?

Conflicts would be difficult enough to manage if they were limited to the bus venue, but as observed by Pam, they permeate the school lives of the kindergartners as well. Walking to class from the bus, I frequently heard the students continuing to struggle with problems or conflicts that began on the bus. These conflicts often find their way into the classroom as well, frequently without any direct resolution.

In one such example, Pablo, a kindergartner, stops by the office on his way to class from the bus one day and reports to the secretary that some older boys were saying "bad words" to him on the bus. The secretary tells Pablo to come back at recess so the principal can help him solve the problem. So Pablo is asked to forestall resolution of his mistreatment for several hours. He is left with no firm, immediate resolution to his predicament and likely feels little sense of support for his troubles on the bus. Pablo is learning that when it comes to the bus venue, he is largely on his own.

For some students, the difficulties on the bus can permeate their in-school experiences in significant ways. For example, for the first several months of school, Felix was so concerned about the bus rides that he would cry nearly every day as he waited for the bus to arrive at the end of the school day. I witnessed Felix's tumult on many occasions. Here is one such example:

> I am waiting at the bus stop with Felix and several other Canford students. The bus is late today, and Felix appears to be getting anxious. After a while I suggest to the group that we go into the office so the secretary can call and find out when the bus will be coming. Felix shakes his head. "No!" he states emphatically. "The bus! The bus!" he calls out and points toward the street. I infer that he wants to stay outside so he can see the bus when it arrives. I tell Felix that he can stay inside with us and watch for the bus through the window, but he refuses to join us and his eyes begin to tear up.
>
> After some continued prodding, Felix eventually follows the group as we go inside to ask the secretary to check the status of the Canford bus. The secretary calls the bus dispatcher and then tells us the bus is on its way. At this point, Felix begins to cry quite fiercely. His body shakes and his shoulders bounce up and down as he emits several loud sobs. I bend down, ask Felix what is wrong, and try to reassure him. Between his tears and sobbing, Felix tells me that he misses his mom, that the bus won't

come, and that he won't make it to Kids' Castle (his after-school program).

"It don' come!" he murmurs as he shakes his head. "It don' come!" Then he adds, "I don' go to Kitscassle [Kids' Castle] and then my Mom don' get me!"

I try to reassure Felix that the bus *will* take him to Kids' Castle and that his mother will come to pick him up, but he is not comforted. Even when the bus finally arrives, Felix remains upset, and he hesitates to get on the bus. The driver is not the one who usually picks him up in the afternoon. Felix stands at the entrance to the bus and shakes his head again. "Where es Ahn-drew?" he asks, looking for his regular driver. Felix is concerned that this driver will not get him to his proper destination. Finally, after some additional assurances, we convince Felix to board the bus, but he is still crying as the bus pulls away from the school.

Felix's worries about the bus begin to affect his daily life at school. At first he gets nervous on the walk to the bus stop. Once he learns the daily routine, he begins to fret about the bus ride during the story time just before dismissal. Felix knows the bus ride is coming, and he peppers his teacher, Allison, with questions and concerns, often interrupting her stories:

"Allison!? When it is the bus time?"
"Allison!? Which bus am I? The 'Z' bus?"
"Allison?! I can get my 'pack-back' now?"

At first, Allison is patient and supportive in dealing with Felix's persistent questions and anxieties about the bus. Eventually, as he continues to interrupt Allison during the group time, she becomes more short with him.

"Can I get my pack-back now?!" Felix calls out. He pauses a moment. "Al-li-sonnn?!" Felix draws out her name. "Can I get my pack-back now?!"
    "No, because we're in the middle of the story, Felix," Allison replies curtly.

Over time, Felix and Allison begin to develop an ongoing conflict during the group times, especially at the end of the day as Felix begins to perseverate on the impending bus ride. Allison also begins to see Felix as a "challenge" and a "handful," as she puts it.

Of course, from time to time, all students bring worries, concerns, and issues from home with them to school. Some of these anxieties are sure to affect their school experiences. This is true not only of Canford students but also of others. Still, for the Canford students, the bus ride imposes one more hurdle to clear, one more venue to grow accustomed to, one more transition to navigate in a complex journey.

Canford students expressed a shared sense of the problematic nature of the bus ride. While on the whole the kindergarten students often had trouble reflecting critically on their school experiences, when it came to the bus rides, the students were clear in their assessments. Here is what some of the Canford students had to say about the bus rides.

Felix (as he looks at a digital photograph of his bus): "You take a picture! How you take a picture? . . . Is that my bus?"

I respond in the affirmative.

"Umm . . . Oh! He picking some kids! In a *big* bus!" (Felix distinguishes this "big" bus, which he rides in the morning, from the smaller bus he rides in the afternoon.)

When I ask what he thinks about the bus, Felix replies, "I don't wanna ride a bus. I don't like it when I ride. I don't like it when I get up early, and my mommy take me to the bus. I don't wanna wake up early."

Paloma: "I like to stay at home. I'm tired to come at school. I don't want to get up early. I wanna stay home wit' my dad. I watch movie and cartoons."

As I walk Callie to class from the bus stop, I ask her, "Do you like to ride on the bus?"

Callie replies, "No. It's scary, so now I go there." She points to the day care center that she attends in the afternoons. I believe her remark is meant to indicate that in the afternoon she doesn't need to ride the bus, because she goes to the after-school program and is then picked up by her mother. I ask Callie if she likes her morning bus rides.

"No," Callie replies. "I just get on it, but I don't like it."

Other student comments reflect this same sentiment:

PALOMA: "It's bad!"
CALLIE: "I don't like it."
HOLLY: "The other kids are mean on the bus."
FELIX: "It wasn't good."

PABLO: "They say bad words [on the bus]."
JOSE: "They was hitting me and calling me names."

For a group of young children who often have difficulty formulating and expressing beliefs and opinions about their own experiences (at least in ways that most grownups can understand), they share a very clear and convincing picture of their school bus rides. The bus rides are early, long, difficult, and disliked.

Round and Round, Round and Round

Transitioning from the bus ride to the classroom can be a complicated task. For some students this adjustment period can be significant, though brief. As one teacher notes, "I think they come in shock from the bus ride, and that wears off after about twenty minutes." For others, like Felix, the period of adjustment can be longer, and for some these tensions and worries can color the entire day. In addition to its impact on the physical condition of the students—the early start and long ride leave many students tired and hungry upon their arrival at school—and the emotional impact of the conflicts and stresses it can produce, the bus ride also has an impact on the general school adjustment and adaptation processes of the Canford students.

> It is 7:55 A.M. The bus arrives at the school a few minutes early today. Aside from the bus driver and me, no adults are present as the students depart from the bus. Alex and Hector get off the bus together and quickly run up the hillside near the bus

stop. The boys run back and forth across the top of the hill, then up and down the steep slope several times in a game of chase. They both appear to be excited and pleased with themselves. They are smiling and laughing as they play. As the only adult present, I once again feel a strain between my researcher and supervisor roles. After watching the boys for several minutes, I sense that they are getting more wound up and are in jeopardy of injuring themselves on the steep hillside. I suggest that they come down from the hill and head toward the classroom. Eventually Alex comes down and begins to wander toward Anita's classroom. Hector follows Alex, and both boys run ahead of me toward the classrooms.

The distance from the hillside to the classroom is perhaps a hundred yards, but it takes the boys a long time to cover this ground. At first, they wander off track. Hector runs past his classroom to a drinking fountain and takes a few sips of water. Alex stands about ten feet from the classroom door as he waits for Hector to return. Then both boys walk around the side of the building and crouch below one of the classroom windows, taking turns to pop up and peer inside. They seem to be trying to hide from view, and they feebly attempt to stifle their giggling as they pop up and down. After watching from a distance for a few minutes, I approach the classroom myself and head through the doorway. As I do so, I pause for a moment, glance at the boys, and smile. They smile back and follow me into the classroom. It is now about 8:05, five minutes after the ringing of the first bell signaling the start of the school day.

In addition to the challenge of getting from the bus to the classroom, another complicating factor is that the bus often arrives to the school late, creating another impediment to a successful and timely transition for the Canford students. On the days that I observed the arrival of the Canford buses, they arrived more than five minutes late more than 40 percent of the time. Given that the transition from the bus stop to the classroom was often a lengthy and unsupervised process, Canford students arrived to class after the morning bell at least half of the time. Because they arrive late so frequently, Canford students often miss a valuable opportunity to acclimate and socialize with peers in the early moments of the school day. In the classrooms I observed, teachers designed various early morning transitional activities specifically to help students adjust to the school setting. For example, in Anita's classroom students could choose from a number of "free choice" activities, including drawing at one of the writing tables, fashioning necklaces out of Cheerios to wear and eat, reading in the classroom library, playing games of checkers, or working with puzzles. In Georgia's classroom, the activities were more structured, reflecting her general teaching style. In the early morning, students would sit at their assigned tables and read books from baskets that Georgia set on the tables before the students' arrival. One feature common to all of the early morning activities was that they were primarily child directed. Even in the more structured settings, the students had a choice of books to peruse or tablemates with whom to read. In addition, and perhaps more important, the morning activities offered students a chance to socialize and interact with classmates, though to varying degrees. Because they were late in arriving, Canford students often missed out on these opportunities.

Following these transitional activities in the morning, the teachers usually moved quickly to a whole-class, teacher-centered event, such as a class meeting. In these settings students had limited participation and firm boundaries on their movements and behaviors. For many students, these extended teacher-centered class meetings were a challenge. Since the bus riders were late to class so frequently, they would often miss the morning transitional activities and join the group at the beginning or in the middle of the teacher-centered class meetings. Coming directly from the rowdy bus ride to a lengthy teacher-centered classroom meeting proved to be a difficult assignment for many of the Canford students, and they were often singled out for reprimands or other forms of negative attention in this setting. Many of these students quickly became tagged as "difficult," and the early morning meetings became a time of conflict between them and their teachers.

The distance between the bus and the classroom, measured not only in space and time but also in terms of the environment and general expectations for behavior, can be quite vast.

All through the Town

Another significant feature of the bus ride is that it highlights the distance between the Canford students and their home communities and families. The mere existence of the busing program is an affirmation of this fact. While the families of participating students make a conscious choice to send their children across town in the hope that they will receive a superior education, the separation may cause some hardships that are worth exploring. In a larger sense the bus acts simultaneously as a bridge to Arbor Town for Canford students and as a moat separating students from their families and their communities.

Because of the distance and time involved, the Canford students can be made to feel isolated and different, making their adjustment to school more difficult than for other students. As Pam states, "I definitely think it's harder for them. Just the . . . bus wise, it's a long trip and, I know, they know that they're different. I'm sure because . . . I just get a sense that they know that, well, I'm a Bus Kid . . . even if it's as simple as, I'm a Bus Kid . . . I take the bus and nobody else does."

Georgia echoes this sentiment: "I think they feel that there's something different because they see everybody else, you know, their parents are here in the morning. I have parents come in and read with the kids, those that can and Pablo's dad does sometimes. He drops him off . . . but usually he takes the bus every morning, like Jose, so his mom never comes in . . . so I'm sure that he must have figured out and said, well, all the other parents are here."

In describing her impressions of the school experience for her Canford students, Anita notes some other distinctions: "One of the things as I was looking at the samples of student work is that other children don't write so much about families, especially Mom. And I think being Bus Kids, they feel so much farther away from Mom and Dad than the kids who live close by, and it must be really scary. So there's that fragile part again, that . . . 'cause they, you know, when you think about it, their only clue to how far away they are is how much time they're in that bus. So they've been in the bus for an hour, that means, well, they might be in . . . New York. [Anita laughs.] You know, far away. And it's a long ride."

The sense of distance and isolation can be exacerbated by conditions at the school site. As Georgia noted, parents would often join her students in the early morning during the transitional reading time. Typically during this time, her three Canford students would be sitting at their tables, leafing through books by themselves. Most of the other children would have parents reading with them or at least helping them to settle into their place before leaving. Georgia would often take the time to assist the Canford students and the others who were unattended, but this early morning experience was clearly significantly different for the two groups of students. Similar scenes played out in the other classrooms I observed, where most neighborhood parents would participate in the morning activities with their children, but where the Canford students' parents would rarely be present.

End of the Line

Being a Bus Kid involves many discomforts. They are subjected to unsupervised and chaotic circumstances on the bus, which is a potentially significant hardship, especially for five- and six-year-olds surrounded by older children. These circumstances give rise to many conflicts and general anxieties about the bus rides. Transitions between the bus rides and school settings can be difficult. Additionally, students who ride the bus are much less likely than neighborhood students to have the immediate support and comfort of a loving parent to help facilitate the morning transition from home to school. As a result, the Canford students can be made to feel isolated and different from their peers.[3]

For Tali, Holly, Paloma, Felix, Alex, Jose, Callie, Pablo, Hector, and others, if being at school often means being tired, hungry, and uncomfortable, then a successful adjustment to this new environment will be even more difficult. All told, such experiences likely contribute to the students coming to school "jangled," the impact of which should not be underestimated. The children, for the most part, are too young to understand the complex factors that help create these circumstances, but they are perceptive enough to recognize that they are not satisfied with the consequences.

IV
Friends

Particularly in the early years, engaging in social interactions and developing and maintaining friendships are arguably two of the primary objectives of schooling, at least from the point of view of the youngsters in the setting.[1] While many school authorities (from federal and state policy makers to local school boards, administrators, and teachers) focus their attention chiefly on the fundamentals of literacy and numeracy, test scores, and national competitiveness, children spend much of their time focused on their peer relationships and social interactions. Even through a cursory experience in a primary school classroom, one can see the strong emphasis, especially on the part of the children themselves, on the making and sorting of friendships and the complications inherent in the social arrangements of childhood.

The Canford students in this study are no exception to this premise. They focus a great deal of their energy and attention in the school setting on forming friendships and finding a successful place among their school peers. That venture is one that the Canford students often find difficult and complex. Finding a central place in the social community of their school peers is something most Canford students struggle with throughout their first year and likely beyond. (Although later years are not within the scope of this project, several teachers and administrators that I interviewed noted that they feel it becomes even more difficult for Canford students to fit in and make social connections as they become older and progress through the school system.)

Further, evidence from the field of educational psychology supports the notion that early successful peer interactions are fundamentally important to future achievement. Early friendship formation and positive social connections at school have been linked to successful school adjustment, future academic success, and general happiness and well-being. Clearly, social relationships are in multiple ways an essential element in the school experience of young children, and they are too often ignored in educational research and policy making.[2]

Consequently, I believe it is worthwhile to take a critical look at the social interactions of the Canford students in developing a picture of their school experience during this first year as they adjust and adapt to their new school environment. A key element in the initial lawsuit and the eventual settlement that brought about the formation of the Canford Program was the hope of providing more integrated social opportunities for the young people in the community at large, in addition to improving educational prospects for those in South Bay City. The experiences of the students in this study speak to those goals as well.

Peripheral Players: Canford Students on the Outside Looking In

How do the Canford students fare in the social realm? With whom do they connect? What kinds of relationships do they develop? How might one characterize the nature of their social roles in their school settings? In general terms the Canford students appear to remain on the periphery, rather than in the center, of the social activity in their school environment. Hector's attempt to connect to his Arbor Town school peers in the sandbox provides an example:

> Hector, a Canford student, is in the sandbox digging by himself. He is working about two feet away from Jack and Cory, two of his Arbor Town school peers, who are working together to dig a large hole.
>
> Jack and Cory carve arrows in the sand directing traffic toward the hole, which they see as a trap. Hector looks over at Jack and Cory every few seconds. They seem to take little note of him. Hector begins to dig arrow-like designs in the sand near his hole as well.
>
> The next time he looks over to the other boys, Hector calls out, "You guys! I did some arrow!"
>
> Without making eye contact, Jack replies, "Gooood, Hec-*thor*." [Jack seems either to feign a slight Spanish accent or to mimic how Hector pronounces his own name.]
>
> Hector turns to me and says, "We're diggin' a hole so Marcos can fall. And William . . . and *you*!" He smiles in my direction. [I note that Hector says "we" though his inclusion in a cooperative project appears doubtful.]
>
> A few moments later, Hector again turns toward Jack and Cory. Hector says, "Hey. Can you guys be my frien'?"
>
> Jack and Cory give no response.
>
> Hector tries again. "Can you guys be my frien'?"

This time Jack responds, "What?"
Hector again asks, "Can you guys be my frien'?"
Jack and Cory make no response. Hector turns
back and continues to dig at his hole alone.

This type of scene was played out again and again during the course of my observations across multiple venues, from the playground to the dramatic play area, table-time activities, class meetings, and more. Hector and his Canford peers were often left on the fringes of events and activities. They seemed most frequently to occupy noncentral roles in social and other domains. In a loose comparison, imagine an archery target consisting of several concentric circles. If one were to characterize the central play occurring among students as the middle circle of the target, Canford students are most often found outside that bull's-eye. While they may enter the central play at times, they do so tentatively and infrequently. Though these students are generally interested in moving toward the center and make repeated efforts to do so, their status as peripheral players within the social network persists.

In contrast to Hector, I would describe Jack and Cory as "central players" in the social realm: students who seem to occupy enviable key roles in play from the perspective of their peers, and who attract the interest and attention of their peers as well. Generally, the central players are students I would describe as being part of the core play on the playground: taking leadership roles, controlling key tools, attracting and directing others, and the like. Taking the kindergarten playground, a key social arena for these students, as an example, centrality might include such practices as the following:

- being actively involved in the social dynamics of dramatic plays by participating, for example, as a crew member of the "spaceship," imagined from the climbing structure;

- taking on the coveted role as the First Boss in a Super Hero Club, directing and orchestrating both the play and the other players;
- assuming a key role in the design and digging of sand castles and creation of waterways;
- maintaining access to essential and scarce tools such as the lone red shovel, a particular pail, or control of the water source;
- achieving desired outcomes in negotiations over turn taking on a slide or a climbing structure.

I liken this notion of centrality to the development of membership in communities of practice, as described by Lave and Wenger (1991). Broadly summarized, this concept illustrates how nascent members of a community, profession, or other group work to move from practicing and learning on the periphery toward more central or expert roles in a community of shared values, understandings, and practices. Lave and Wenger note that some such apprenticeships are more effective than others. I believe that this concept also provides a useful framework in thinking about the Canford students in the school setting and their often ineffective and unsupported efforts to move from peripheral participation to more central roles in various venues in the school setting. Hector, like many students in his class, likes to be included in play with Jack and Cory. He clearly has an interest in finding a way toward the center of social play but is frequently unable to gain access to that space and opportunity. Unfortunately, such exclusion is a common feature in the social lives of the Canford students in this study.

Of course, there are few, if any, children who command a central role in every venue at all times. Roles and boundaries are often fluid in these kinds of settings, especially with children in this age group. Still, I would characterize the central players as those who comfortably command central and near-central roles in many venues and who frequently interact with other key players. Centrality is a label I would ascribe infrequently to the Canford students.

Feeling Left Out

Though the Canford children seem pretty happy, I still get a feeling that they don't truly feel a part of things.
—*Georgia, an Arbor Town kindergarten teacher*

One of the many ways I tried to learn about the school lives of the young children in my study was to conduct storytelling interviews. With the permission of their teacher, previous consent of their parents, and their own capacity to decline or accept my offer, I asked the children if they would like to accompany me and do some special storytelling activities together. I provided the children with a large piece of white drawing paper and a set of colored markers and crayons. Then I told the children that I wanted to learn more about their school and that a fun way to do so would be for them to draw a picture and tell me a story about school. As they dictated, I typed their words into my laptop computer. Once they were finished, I read the stories back to them, and later I would print and affix the stories to their illustrations. The children all appeared to find the process enjoyable, and they expressed pleasure in hearing their own words repeated to them as a "real story" at the end of the process. These stories provided some insights into the thoughts, feelings, and ideas that the children had about schooling and many other topics they chose to focus on as well.[3]

Interestingly, but perhaps not too surprisingly, most of the stories the children shared were about friends: making friends, playing with friends, adventuring with friends, arguing with and solving problems with friends. There were numerous accounts with a general focus on friends and friendships, such as stories about playing with friends on the playground or having adventures with friends. Additionally, many of the Canford students' stories expressed particular worries and concerns that the children had about their connections with peers. These included stories about arguing with potential friends or stories about having difficulty finding friends with whom to play.

Felix's story, "Hide and Seeks," for example, is a general account of his friendships at school:

HIDE AND SEEKS

by Felix

I like drawing and playing with my friends. And I have six [meaning he's six years old]. And I play with my friends. They're so nice. Andy and Jeff T. and Kevin and Byron and Jack and Dustin and Paloma and Alfonzo and Roman and Steven and Alexander and Andrew, Matthew and Danielle and Marble Run and Tire Swing. That's all my friends. Jack and Dustin tried to find us but they couldn't. But they saw Andy and Byron first. And then nothing.

In this storytelling episode Felix lists his sixteen "friends" (including Marble Run and Tire Swing, which are actually favored activities rather than individuals), yet based on my observations and the concurrence of his teacher, in practice Felix has few close friends at school. While this tale of friendship far exceeds Felix's actual daily interactions with peers, at the same time it expresses some of his hopes and desires in that realm. Like most children, Felix strongly desires the friendship of his peers. Accomplishing that aim, however, proves elusive.

Hector's story, "My School," is an example of the stories that hint at some of the worries and concerns the children have about their connections with their peers:

MY SCHOOL

by Hector

This is the tree house and they are fighting me because I'm not getting up so fast to the tree house. And then I call them, "Okay, I will go on so fast," and I did go on so fast. And then they said, "Don't play in the doll house, play on the table. Color." And I did. And then they said "Hector, hurry, they're almost gonna ring the bell, and we're almost gonna go outside!" and then we went outside. And we played tire swing. The end.

Here we can sense Hector's urgency to join the group. In his story Hector is making every effort to do what he feels is required to be a part of the central play, but his attempts always seem to be one step short. This story reflects Hector's efforts to fit in in school and on the playground, where in spite of his efforts, he often finds himself on the outside, as do many of his Canford peers.

On other occasions and in various other ways, Canford students expressed their frustrations at the difficulty they encountered in making strong social connections at school. Callie's experience of isolation and disconnect is one that is shared among many of her Canford peers—a reaction, I believe, to the peripheral nature of their participation in social networks.

It is late February, during the morning recess break. The students begin their morning recess with a snack at the picnic tables near their classrooms. Delia, the teacher, sets a timer to ring after ten minutes, signaling to the students they may pack up their snacks and leave for the playground. At the first sound of the bell, most of the students grab their lunch bags, run to drop them off in the baskets near their classrooms, and quickly dart toward the kindergarten play area.

Callie is still eating her snack. She has an abundance of food in her bag: a donut, a bag of chips, two juice boxes, a sandwich, and more. After another five minutes pass, Callie is the last student remaining at the picnic tables. I often find her sitting by herself, and she is frequently the last to leave for the playground. Delia asks her to put her snack away so she'll have time to play, but Callie says she needs to eat the whole snack or her mom will say something about it. Delia suggests that Callie leave what she doesn't want so that Mom will know how much to pack next time. Callie decides to stay at the snack table. Delia says, "Okay, a few more minutes, then it's time to clean up and go out to play."

"Well, no one will want to be my friend," Callie says under her breath. It is unclear if Delia hears her. She offers no response as she heads inside for her own recess break.

I walk near Callie's table on my way to the playground, and she asks me to stay with her as she finishes her snack. I oblige, and we begin to talk about what Callie has brought for snack today and about her day at school. Callie then asks me a few questions about my day and what my daughter likes to eat for snack. I steer our conversation to the topic of friendship, and I ask Callie if she has any new friends at school.

"A little bit," Callie says.

"Why don't you tell me about them?" I ask.

Callie then tells me about some of her South Bay City friends and her cousins that she likes to play with at home. Then I ask again about her friends from school.

"Eleanor," Callie offers, noting one of her classmates. "Yesterday [Sunday] she wanted me to go swimming with her." [I am a bit dubious of Callie's claim, as I have not heard of this play opportunity from any other source, nor have I known of any play opportunities between Callie and her school peers outside of the school setting. I do know from other conversations and my observations that Eleanor is someone whom Callie would like to have as a friend.]

I ask Callie about her other friends at school. Callie gives no response.

Then I ask more specifically, "Who do you like to play with at recess?"

Callie says, "I like to play with you."

"What if I'm not here?" I ask.

Callie points to herself and smiles.

"You like to play with Callie?" I ask.

Callie nods in the affirmative. "My heart," she says, continuing to point in that general direction.

Once she finally makes it out to the play area for recess, Callie bounces between the garden area and other settings on the playground, such as the climbing structure and a picnic table set up for drawing. She plays independently, moving from one venue to another every few minutes, often returning to wander solo around the gardening beds between flurries of interaction at other sites. At one point Callie sees Alana, a second grader who rides the SBC bus with Callie in the mornings. Callie runs out of the kindergarten play area and chases Alana briefly before returning to the kindergarten play structure. This is her first and only interaction with another student during recess today, and it is a pattern I see repeated frequently.

While Callie is perhaps the most disconnected of the Canford students in my study, her experience of isolation is familiar to other Canford students. Comments in interviews and general conversations with the Canford students reflect their sense of exclusion from the core social play at school:

MARIKIT: "No one would let me play with them."

JOSE: "I like to play with Steven, but he doesn't like to play with me."

FELIX: "I just play with myself."

Like Callie, many of the Canford students spent much of their outdoor time at what I termed a "home base" site: a location where they played alone but also seemed to feel comfortable and safe. While Callie used the garden as a safe space to which she could retreat, Marikit's home base was the monkey bars; Cherise's home base was under the branches of a large oak tree; Hector clung to the teaching assistant from his class, often engaging her in a game of chase. From their home base the students would then venture forth to play in other settings, often returning to their home base after brief encounters with other children. While this strategy may have assisted the students in gaining a sense of comfort and control over their social environment, it also tended to keep them isolated and disconnected from their school peers.

Occasional episodes of loneliness or doubts about acceptance are certainly experiences shared by many young children. Yet the pattern is a consistent and prevalent one for the Canford students, one that makes up a significant portion of their school lives in the social realm. As the students' stories and my observations reveal, in attempting to connect to the social worlds of their kindergarten peers, Canford students are often found on the outside looking in.

Beyond School Opportunities

Several factors appear to be at work in limiting the social connections between Canford students and their Arbor Town school peers. For example, Felix's teacher, Allison, notes how her Canford students begin school without any close connections, a situation that persists to some degree over the course of the year: "I think a lot of [neighborhood] kids know each other already. But Felix was coming in not knowing anybody, and I think he was scared. . . . Felix probably didn't have any real close buddies. He made connections with a wide group in the classroom, but no close connections. . . . Some kids, they would use him to do things that they didn't want to do. Like Andy would say 'Go get the watering can,' and Felix would do it. So I think that he was 'friends' with Andy a lot, because Felix would do what he said. He was getting along with everybody, but he didn't have any close friends. . . . It was hard for him." As this teacher suggests, the Canford students come to school in unfamiliar territory with few, if any, social connections, and likely without an understanding of many of the shared rules and community practices that might help them to adapt or adjust with relative ease.

So this pattern of separation really begins prior to the inception of the school year. Further, it is exacerbated by the Canford students' diminished opportunities for interaction with their school peers beyond the school day. As Georgia, another teacher, points out, "That's really our first job of the year, is making friends and everything. And . . . um . . . it was hard for Jose to feel like he was really, you know, connected. When you go home and you don't see anybody [from school], you don't have play dates, this is the only place you see them, it's hard to make friends."

Thus, for some students social relationships in school are supported and fostered by opportunities for students to connect outside of school. For Canford students, though, many factors work together to make such outside-of-school connections difficult. First, while many neighborhood students enjoy social relationships with future elementary school peers before kindergarten (through local preschools, neighborhood activities, and shared playground use, for example), such interactions are quite uncommon for Canford students. In addition, the geographic distance between Arbor Town and South Bay City makes play dates difficult. Since most Canford students rely

on the bus for transportation, they are often generally un-
available after school. Cultural and linguistic differences
among families are also a factor. Not surprisingly, parents
who do not speak the same language or share personal connections themselves find it more difficult to help their children connect socially.

Freda, a language tutor who works with many of the
Canford students, summarizes the issues succinctly:

> I think it is very difficult for them [Canford stu-
> dents] to integrate into the community and with
> the other students, because there is such a big dif-
> ference in families from here and from South Bay
> City. In many cases I tried to help families to get to-
> gether, but what happens is the family here [in
> Arbor Town] doesn't speak Spanish, and the family
> from South Bay City doesn't speak English at all.
> So, maybe once you can make an arrangement, but
> it's not going to keep happening, because they can-
> not depend on you all the time, and it doesn't work
> well. And then, sometimes some of the Canford stu-
> dents played with a friend here, and of course they're
> coming from a very tiny apartment where there are
> eight or ten people living together, and they go
> here to Arbor Town, and they see this mansion, and
> it's a total shock for them, because they have never
> seen that before. I think they feel . . . I don't know,
> uneasy. So it is difficult for them in a social way. I
> don't think they integrate.

In addition to missing out on play dates, Canford students and their families participate less frequently in other
school-related activities, such as school picnics, open house

nights, and birthday parties with classmates. The point here is not that Canford students do not engage in activities outside school that are rewarding and important, just that they participate in fewer events related to school and involving school peers outside of school. Again, issues of timing, transportation, geography, culture, language, and the like are all at play, keeping many Canford students and families on the outside of the social scene, rather than in the center. This separation underscores how difficult it can be for these students and their families to become comfortable and feel a part of the larger school community. As a further complication, some district teachers tend to equate Canford parents' lack of participation in school functions with a general lack of interest in or commitment to the educational endeavors of their children. This perception further exacerbates the situation of social distance or disconnect. As one teacher notes, missing out on after-school events "often would set kids apart, you know, the Canford kids would never come to any Kinder Coffees [a recurring opportunity for the children in her class to do small performances and for parents to socialize]. It was always like, the other kids would say, 'so-and-so isn't here,' and I would have to say, 'Well, he probably couldn't come tonight, so we'll just do the play without them.'"

Birthday parties are an especially important social occasion in the world of young children. Being invited to and attending the birthday parties of peers is a barometer of inclusion among schoolchildren. The obstacles noted above in relation to play dates and after-school events apply to this realm as well, affecting another significant social opportunity for the Canford students. On two separate occasions, Cherise feels the impact of being unable to participate with her school peers in this important rite of passage:

Early one Monday morning, Cherise arrives at school looking dejected. I ask her about her weekend, and she says, "No one [from school] came to my birthday party. They were all busy. I invited that Melody," she says, pointing to one of her school peers, "and now she won't even talk to me!" The tension between the girls has developed as Cherise confronted Melody upon arriving at school, asking her why she hadn't attended her birthday party.

On a separate occasion, we see Cherise feeling left out of a special birthday event:

Cherise arrives at school with a handmade crown that she presents to Emily. Cherise had been invited to Emily's birthday party over the weekend, but she was unable to attend. As Emily talks to her peers at school about the party, including details of pony rides, balloons, and a birthday cake, Cherise listens in, clearly captivated by Emily's descriptions. At the conclusion of the narrative, Cherise folds her arms and abruptly slaps them down across her chest. With a forced frown on her face, and a mock stomp of her foot, she expresses her regret at having missed Emily's party.

Such events clearly have a strong impact on students' sense of belonging and connection to their school peers, which affects other aspects of their school experience as well. Several comments from teachers underscore this trend of social isolation and its influence on the Canford students. In an end-of-year interview, Pablo's teacher, Georgia, looks back on his school year with guarded optimism: "He seems like a happy kid, and he seems like he likes school. I don't know. He seems like he had a good year." At the same time, she notes some difficulties that he and his Canford peers had in making social connections: "I don't know about play dates. I see a lot of students going home with other ones, and I never see Pablo or the other Canford students going home with anyone else." When she looks ahead at the prospects for Pablo and Jose (two Canford students), she notes the importance of their enhancing social connections: "My hope for them would be to socially get more involved, you know, with the other kids. Which, I'm sure they will, because they'll be in a whole new mix. So just making more friends, for both of them. 'Cause comparatively, I would say, you know, more of the other kids have closer friends. . . . I don't know. The thing I see is play dates going on. That kind of bothers me that they [Canford students] don't have play dates with their classmates. . . . But that would be my one concern, just kinda mixing more in."

Another teacher expresses some hope, in part, that her Canford students will fare better socially in the coming year, but her own experience with former Canford students portends a less optimistic fate: "So, I had one Canford student who was African American and he did great, wonderfully [academically], like he was pretty much one of the top readers, you know? He's in first grade now and he was, I mean, socially fine last year. He made friends. The thing is, after-school play dates never happened, though, which is sad because it's hard, it never happened, not once. But, socially, in here, he was fine. But now, in first grade his teacher said he's having problems connecting."

As one other teacher notes, "Yeah, that sort of feeds into another thing too, a big one. It happens so many times. Cedric came to me so many times last year and said, 'When can I have a play date?' But it never happened, you know, because the boundary is rarely, rarely crossed."

Built in part on the hopes of a more integrated social and academic community, the Canford Program will likely achieve its ideals only by making connections both in and beyond the school context. Play dates and other opportunities to socialize with school peers beyond the school setting, or the lack of these possibilities, have a clear impact on the lives of the Canford students.

Developing Social Relationships

Roland Tharp and his colleagues developed a framework they titled the "Great Cycle of Social Sorting" to explain the development of relationships and friendships in society and its impact on relationships in the school setting (Tharp et al., 2000). In common terms, they describe how social connections require opportunities to spend time together ("propinquity") as well as opportunities to work together toward common, meaningful goals ("joint productive activity"). By working together toward common objectives, individuals build connections and shared perspectives ("intersubjectivity"). This in turn fosters a mutual attraction and a greater desire to spend more time together ("affinity"). People who share an affinity for one another are likely to spend more time together ("propinquity"), and so the cycle continues.

Clearly one of the issues at play here for the Canford students is propinquity. They have many fewer opportunities to interact with their Arbor Town peers outside of school than those students do with one another. This process begins before the start of elementary school, and once kindergarten begins, the Canford students spend a great deal of their outside-of-school time on the bus, in on- and off-site day care settings, and in their home communities. (I will also argue in a later chapter that some teachers afford very few *in-school* opportunities to build such connections.) Without the key ingredient of propinquity, strong social connections are unlikely to develop.

If we think again about the peripheral nature of the Canford students in the school's social scene, broader outside-of-school connections could provide one means of assisting them in gaining a foothold in the center of social play. Their limited interactions with school peers, both in and outside of the school setting, exacerbate the peripheral nature of their standing in the school's social setting.

In spite of the obstacles mentioned above, some parents and teachers do strive to connect and include Canford students in after-school activities. Some play dates are arranged, much to the delight of the students. Often an entire class is invited to a birthday party, though Canford students still have a more difficult time attending. Yet some parents and teachers make an extra effort to help Canford students connect to their school peers and feel part of the school community. Still, the results of these efforts are tenuous and hard to sustain.

Anita describes some of the efforts the parents in her classroom took to include Canford students in after-school social activities: "We have a proactive group of parents this year, in terms of inclusion in social functions. The other day I was meeting with my lead room parent and two other parents, and they all are Spanish speakers! Steve has said he will be a liaison for Hector's family. . . . I met with Hector's family just before my meeting with Steve and the others. When the meeting with Hector's family was over, all the families talked together in Spanish. From what I gather, there is genuine interest from these parents to get the Canford children to the parties."

Georgia discusses efforts by another family to include Canford students in a birthday celebration: "As for Pablo, Jose, and Juan, they were all invited personally by Drew's mom [to his birthday party]. I know Jose did not attend. I don't know about the other two. Doug, Lisa's dad, called Pablo's family also. Doug is a really socially conscious person, and he believes people from the west side of the freeway need to make some appearances over in the east side. I wish I could think of a way to facilitate that."

In spite of the good intentions of some parents and teachers, maintaining these connections proves problematic. Another teacher describes the difficulty of sustaining these social connections outside of school:

> When it does happen [play dates], they come here [Canford students tend to come to Arbor Town]. They are invited to the families here and it's only families with really golden hearts . . . These parents really listen to us when we say something like . . . I mentioned to them that it was a goal of mine to get the kids really integrated and the only way that happens, I think, is through play dates. Maybe it's not the only way, but it's a powerful way, so they've gone out of their way to make sure those kids are invited to parties and given rides, but it never goes the other way, and the kids aren't invited over there, and I don't know if all the parents are comfortable with it—if they feel comfortable crossing that line. Mostly what my students have done in the past was set up play dates at parks and things like that. But most of the time, it's a one-time occurrence and it's hard to reorganize. It doesn't seem like they actu-

ally can foster some kind of long-term friendships
or relationships that way.

Interpersonal connections among parents play a large
role in facilitating such relationships, especially with young
children. Many teachers provide opportunities for parents to
participate in transitional activities in the classrooms at the
beginning of the day. Parents connect to their children *and* to
one another during these morning transitions. In addition,
parents who pick up their children after school have numerous
informal opportunities to make their own social connections
and to support and encourage their children in developing
play dates and social opportunities after school. A quick trip
after class to the school playground by two classmates, whose
parents are spending time talking together, can go a long way
toward fostering further social connections. These opportunities allow parents to become comfortable with one another
and with having their children supervised by the other parents. Informal connections among the adults provide the social oil that facilitates the children's connections, play dates,
and possible friendships. In a sense, the neighborhood parents
have their own opportunities for propinquity and to build
affinity, developing their own social ties and connections at the
school site. Canford students and families are largely left out of
this informal system.

Consequences of Being Outsiders

Although forming strong social bonds and entering the core
social play with Arbor Town classmates is difficult for Canford
students, they still have rich and complex social lives at school
that are characterized in three important ways. First, Canford

students tend to associate most closely with students on the periphery of social activity, primarily other Canford students but also other "outsiders" in the social scene. Second, students on the periphery often compete with one another in their attempts to gain access to scarce spaces in the social center. Finally, such conflicts and connections with other outsiders often support and encourage the development of behaviors that are viewed negatively by both teachers and school peers, further pushing the Canford students away from the social center.

RESEGREGATION AND CONNECTION TO OTHER OUTSIDERS

The Canford students' primary social connections at schools are with other outsiders. Georgia describes the developing friendships of three Canford students, Pablo, Jose, and Christopher. Pablo and Jose are both students in Georgia's classroom, and Christopher is a Canford peer in another kindergarten class. Early in the year Georgia notes the difficulties Jose has in making connections on the play yard, then later in the year she discusses how he has joined his Canford peers in forming a social network: "Outside, Jose is miserable, I think. He was just sad the whole time because nobody would play with him, and then I found that he really likes Pablo. And Pablo likes Jose in here [in the classroom], but then when they go outside, Pablo and Christopher are friends. Christopher doesn't like Jose, so then they wouldn't play with Jose and so he would be, just so sad and didn't want to play with really anybody else."

Even later in the year, Georgia provides an update on these relationships. She notes that the Canford students are still primarily connecting with one another. In addition, Pablo has recently connected with a new student, another outsider: "As for friends, he [Pablo] had . . . a lot of people like him in the class. We have a new boy, Paul [a neighborhood student], and he calls Pablo 'my buddy.' They sit next to each other, which probably helped that friendship, but they're really good friends. Um . . . Jose and Pablo are good friends. Pablo and Christopher play together a lot outside. So I'd say most of his friends are from the Canford Program, but he did have Paul." Christopher's teacher provides a similar assessment: "Also, the beginning of the year was hard for Christopher. Outside, he didn't have anybody to play with. I tried to encourage my other kids to play with him more. But he kinda naturally just hung out with Pablo. . . . Now, I think it's pretty well taken care of. Jose, Pablo, and Christopher now all play together."

The other Canford students demonstrated a similar pattern. Although they sometimes interacted and connected with other school peers, their primary relationships were most often formed with other Canford students or, at times, with other outsiders.

Some Canford students, like Christopher, make their closest connections with Canford peers from other classes. These may be students that they know from their community or from the bus rides, and they connect at school primarily during common outdoor times. In the narrative below, for example, Cherise complains about her lack of friends in her classroom but expresses delight in seeing one of her friends from the bus:

> I see Cherise climbing by herself, not too engaged in any particular activities today. I ask, "Who are you going to play with today?"
> "By myself," Cherise says.

"Why?" I ask.

"Because I don't have no friends," she replies.

"Who would you like to play with?" I ask.

"Amy," Cherise says, and she smiles broadly as she points to the "Big Kids' Playground."

"Do you see that girl with the pink jacket? That's her," she says.

"Where do you know her from?" I ask.

"She's my friend. We ride on the bus together," Cherise tells me.

"Do you have any friends in your class?" I ask.

"No," Cherise says. "Do you want to play with me?" she asks.

"Sure," I say, and at Cherise's suggestion, we begin a game of hide and seek.

Cherise feels more closely connected to students with whom she rides the bus than to her classmates. This was true of many of the Canford students: they found their closest connections with other Canford students, even ones outside of their own classroom or grade level. This pattern was generally uncommon in the kindergarten classrooms in which I worked, where most close friendships were formed within the confines of the classroom, a logical outgrowth of the students' general separation by class group during their school day. The fact that some of the Canford students built their primary social relationships outside of their classroom peer group underscores the forces pushing toward their resegregation in the schools.

Connecting and relating to program peers is not a problem in and of itself. In fact, there are surely some benefits to having friends with whom one shares common and significant experiences, not to mention cultural and linguistic practices.

For example, relationships with program peers may provide a source of comfort, companionship, and social engagement, or an opportunity to comfortably express native language and cultural practices in an unfamiliar setting. In addition, because the Canford students share many features of their school experience, they can provide useful resources and support structures for one another in their efforts to navigate this schooling experience outside of their own communities. Other benefits may be relevant as well. Still, the tendency for students to resegregate represents a lost opportunity—not only for the Canford students, I would add—particularly relevant to a program built as the product of a racial discrimination and desegregation lawsuit.

COMPETITION AND INFIGHTING ON THE PERIPHERY

The children appear to view centrality and social connections with school peers as a scarce resource, something to be hoarded rather than shared.[4] As an ironic consequence, while the Canford students tend to resegregate socially in the Arbor Town schools, as perennial outsiders they also frequently fight with one another for access to central roles or central players. In so doing, they often hurt the ones with whom they are most closely connected. Relationships in this setting and in this age group are complex, fluid, and dynamic. Students connect in play settings, disengage, and reconnect in other ways with great frequency. I would often find a group of students arguing and bullying one another under the play structure, and then gleefully playing a game of hide-and-seek soon thereafter.

As an example, Felix and Oscar—Canford students, classmates, and friends—had a difficult time engaging successfully with their Arbor Town classmates. At the same time, they constantly battled with one another in their efforts to achieve some level of success in the social realm:

> During snack time, Felix and Oscar are sitting across from one another at the same picnic table. They have been arguing throughout the snack period, grabbing dishes from one another, speaking aggressively, and generally giving each other a hard time.
>
> At one point, Felix says to Oscar, "You don't got no friends! You don't got no friends!" To emphasize his point about Oscar's ineptitude, Felix points to the cream cheese bowl and shouts, "You don't even know how to do that!" indicating that Oscar does not know how to properly spread the cream cheese on his bagel.
>
> "Yes, I do have friends! *You* don't have no friends," Oscar calls back.
>
> "Well, no one talks to you," Felix says, at which point the teacher comes by to talk to the boys.

Later Oscar and Felix have a similar exchange on the playground:

> Oscar and Terry are working together to build sand castles. Terry, a neighborhood student, is one of the social leaders among the boys in the class. As he walks by the area, Felix steps on one of Oscar's sand castles. Oscar yells, "No!" and shoots an angry look in Felix's direction.
>
> Felix and Oscar then initiate a vociferous argument about Terry and whose friend he is.

"No, he's my frien'. We making san-cassles," Oscar states, claiming Terry as his friend because they are building in the sand together.

Felix responds by shouting, "He's *my* friend! I see him at the store, 'member?" He glances at Terry as he lays claim to his friendship by virtue of their encounter outside of school.

The argument escalates and the boys begin grabbing and pushing. The teacher intervenes and removes both boys from the sandbox for a brief chat, taking both of them away from their coveted peer.

I found it painful to watch these students, who were already clearly discomforted by their social difficulties, choose to direct some of their frustration toward one another.

Christopher's story, "Me and Pablo Were Mad," further illustrates this issue:

ME AND PABLO WERE MAD

by Christopher

Once when me and Pablo fell down, he say, "Why you hit me?"

And I say, "It was an accident."

"It was not an accident," said Pablo. And we were fighting.

The teacher were coming.

"Let's play now," he said.

And we beed good friends. The end.

In story form Christopher shares a common experience in his social relationships with his peers. He is often trying to balance pushing his Canford peers away and keeping them close as friends. Christopher often argues and fights with Pablo, especially if the possibility of engaging central players emerges. Yet they remain buddies throughout the year, and Christopher does not have any closer friends at school than Pablo.

Christopher clearly wants to be a part of the core social group in his classroom. He dotes on peers such as Patrick and David, two popular classmates, following their lead in choosing activities and frequently beseeching them to join him in play. He often rejects his own Canford peers and friends in favor of the possibility of connecting with these more central players in his class, though success in this enterprise comes infrequently.

> After Pam finishes reading the class a story, she dismisses students to "free choice" activities. Pam asks students to raise their hands and share with her their activity choice, after which she releases students to their selected activities.
>
> Christopher rises up from the floor onto his knee. He raises his hand high in the air and shakes his finger rapidly back and forth. His eyes open wide and he leans forward as he tries to gain Pam's attention.
>
> Pam selects Christopher first and asks him what activity he would like to do. "Playhouse!" Christopher calls out eagerly as he stands up and begins to trot toward the Playhouse area.
>
> A few moments later Christopher jogs back to the rug area and announces, "Patrick wants to come too!" Clearly Christopher *wants* Patrick to join him at the playhouse, but Patrick has already chosen to play with the blocks.

"I think Patrick wants to do the blocks," Pam says.

Christopher pauses and looks longingly at Patrick. "I want to do blocks too," he says. Pam reminds Christopher that he has already selected the Playhouse and that the block area is currently "full." (Pam allows only a certain number of students at each activity center during choice time.)

Christopher wanders back to the Playhouse. No other students have chosen to join him yet. He perfunctorily begins to rearrange the kitchen toys on the play oven and the small, round table, while peering out into the room. He seems to be looking for someone else to play with him in the Playhouse. Eventually he spies David, who is wandering by.

"David, will you play with me?" Christopher asks.

"No, I'm doing computers," David responds.

Meanwhile, Cherise, one of Christopher's Canford peers, volunteers to join Christopher in the Playhouse:

"I'll play," Cherise offers.

Christopher does not respond.

Sitting near the two, I chime in and say, "Cherise would like to join you, Christopher."

"But we don't need a sister," Christopher protests, and he continues to arrange a meal at the table while searching the room for other companions.

Emily walks by and Christopher asks her to join him in the Playhouse. Emily, a neighborhood student, declines.

Noting Christopher's increasing disappointment and frustration, I offer to join him in the play, but for now Christopher does not count me as a worthy play peer, either. He looks skeptically at me and grins. "Nahh," he says as he shakes his head.

Cherise, though, is happy to have a playmate, and she asks me to bake a pretend cake for her birthday, which I do. Christopher eventually engages us as well, though the enthusiasm with which he initially made the choice to come to the Playhouse has been lost.

This episode is interesting for many reasons. Christopher and most of the other Canford students are desperate to make connections to their school peers, especially ones they see as central players. This is evidenced in particular as Christopher rejects Cherise, purportedly because he doesn't need a "sister" for his play, yet he quickly turns to Emily and invites her to join in instead. Emily, like David and Patrick, is both one of the central players and a neighborhood student in Christopher's class. Cherise and I fit neither description.

A similar situation happens on the playground between two Canford students, Cherise and Callie. While neither of them has someone to play with, Callie rejects Cherise as a worthy play partner and in the process highlights some deeper elements in this drama:

It is recess time, and all of the students are on the play yard. Callie and Cherise are both by themselves. Callie is walking along the garden, near me, and Cherise is climbing on the play structure alone. Cherise reaches the crest of the arched steps to the bridge and pauses. Her expression is downcast.

I walk over toward the structure and ask Cherise, "What are you doing?"

"Nothing," Cherise says.

"Nothing?!" I say. "What would you like to play?"

"No one would let me play with them," Cherise says mournfully.

Callie has wandered into the vicinity as well, and I say to both of the girls, "You two could play together."

"I don't play with black kids," Callie says. (Both Callie and Cherise are African American.)

"Why?" I ask.

"I hate them," Callie says. "They do too many stupid things. Like boards." [I think she means "boring" here, though I'm not sure.] Callie walks away. I stay and engage Cherise and offer to play with her. Eventually, we begin a game of chase together.

Why doesn't Callie wish to engage Cherise as a playmate? Clearly there are issues in play beyond the rejection of a peer on the periphery, though this episode fits this pattern of social behavior. Callie has begun to identify Cherise, and perhaps herself, as an unworthy playmate based at least in part on her racial identification. How and where did Callie develop this perspective, and what else is at play here? Has Callie begun to connect her peripheral status with her developing racial identity? Callie and Cherise are the only African American students in their respective classes, and they are among only a handful of black students at the school site. It is reasonable to imagine that a heightened awareness of their minority status in this setting has an impact on their self-perception and their perception of their peers, as well as on their school experiences more broadly conceived. The impact of the interactions of race, language, culture, and social dynamics on the experience of the Canford students is complex and critical, but it does not seem to be acknowledged or confronted in a comprehensive fashion by the attendant schools and educators.

A related strategy for the peripheral players appeared to be one of mistreating other students on the periphery in order to gain the approval and possible acceptance of central players in an activity. As the following narrative demonstrates, the students perhaps sense that harassing other outsiders could be a possible inroad to the social center. Alternatively, this may be a tactic used to deflect frustration at being left out of the social center. Whatever the rationale, I often observed the peripheral students engaged in episodes of infighting such as the one described here:

> During "free choice" time, Pablo moves to the building area where students have access to materials such as blocks, Legos, connecting cubes, cars, and the like. Ian and Adam (both neighborhood students and central players) are already building a complex set of towers and buildings. As usual, they seem to be in command of the building area. They have taken up much of the center workspace and have control of a large portion of the key building materials, as well as the most sought after cars and trucks. Pablo sets to work on one side of Adam and Ian. He begins to build a tower as well, and he looks over at Adam and Ian frequently as he builds. From time to time, Pablo reaches over and takes some of the loose materials that are within reach of Adam and Ian but have not yet been put to use. As he does so, he glances up at the other boys, perhaps looking

for a reaction of some kind or to see if they will notice. Pablo seems unsure whether he can have access to the materials within Adam and Ian's purview.

A few feet away, Daren (a neighborhood student but also an outsider in the group) is building his own tower. He talks to himself as he works. Daren seems to take little note of the other boys at this point. Socially and physically less mature than the other boys in the class, Daren often works alone.

I sit down next to Pablo and build a rectangular "pool" near Pablo's tower. Pablo asks if he can use the pool I'm building, and I agree. Adam then suggests that he and Ian connect their buildings to Pablo's, and Pablo readily assents. As they begin to work together, Adam tells Pablo that he doesn't want to connect his buildings with Daren's, and he tells Pablo not to work with Daren either.

A short while later, Jose (another Canford student) comes to work in the building area too. He sits down next to Pablo and begins to take some of the blocks near Pablo to make a tower. As he reaches for one of the longer blocks, Pablo grabs it and says, "No! I'm using it!" Pablo pulls the block out of Jose's reach.

Jose uses other blocks to build a small tower. He leans over onto his knees toward Adam and Pablo and says, "I'll help you guys."

Pablo replies with a curt, "No!" and he continues to work with Adam.

At this point, Jose slaps down one of Pablo's towers and yells out, "You're mean!"

Pablo responds by yelling back, "Well, *you're* mean for knocking my tower down!"

Perhaps as a reaction to his own sense of being left out of the central play or perhaps in an attempt to get back in, Jose then begins to torment Daren:

After being rejected by Pablo, Jose begins to build on his own again, sitting between Daren and the other boys. Daren says to Jose, "These are the good guys and these are the bad guys," pointing to two different colored sets of bears he has lined up around his tower.

"You're a bad guy, and I'm a good guy," Jose says to Daren. Daren is frequently involved in dramatic play with "good guys" and "bad guys" and Jose knows that Daren emphatically does not like to be a "bad guy."

Daren responds to Jose's taunt by shouting back, "No! I'm a good guy! I'm a good guy!"

Jose watches Daren's reaction and calmly leans over and begins to take some of the blocks that Daren is using, including some that are already a part of Daren's structure. This action clearly upsets Daren further. He begins to shake his hands up and down and calls out, "No, Jose! Don't!" Jose stops for a time, but as soon as Daren turns away, he pulls more blocks from Daren's tower.

Once he notices Jose's continued pilfering, Daren begins to get hysterical. He starts crying and yelling at Jose. "No, Jose! Nooo!"

From across the room, Georgia (the teacher) calls over, "Okay boys, it's time to clean up."

Jose gets up quickly, walks over to Pablo's tower, and knocks it down while Pablo's back is turned. With an angry look on his face, Pablo turns around quickly toward Jose.

"Adam did it," Jose says, and both boys glance at Adam.

Adam looks back at the boys and says, "No, Daren did it!" Adam points at Daren and smiles at Pablo and Jose, both of whom smile back, and all of the boys nod their heads in affirmation.

The Canford students were frequently willing to exclude or fight one another or other outsiders for spaces closer to the social center. They also chose to focus negative attention and behaviors on other outsiders in the hopes of gaining attention from and access to more central figures. Each of these strategies is employed at some point in the narrative above. First, while Pablo is successful in gaining access to play in the social center with Adam and Ian, he shuts down Jose's efforts to follow suit. Jose's first reaction is to express his discontent with Pablo, knocking down his tower. Being unable to control events in the social center, Jose asserts his power over his peer in the periphery: Jose focuses his attention on Daren, disrupting Daren's play and causing Daren great distress. Additionally, we see at the end of this episode that Jose's efforts are somewhat rewarded in this regard, as all of the boys join together in their conspiracy to blame Daren for knocking over Pablo's tower. In this brief moment, Jose and Pablo both share a scene in the social center with Adam and Ian at Daren's expense.

Antagonistic Behaviors Lead to Negative Attention

A final note in regard to this pattern of competition and in-fighting among the Canford students is that it tends to shine a negative spotlight on the children who employ it. After the episode described above, for example, Daren expressed the difficulties he'd had with Jose in the block area to Georgia, who in turn reprimanded Jose and made him apologize and help Daren clean up his blocks. Perhaps this was a reasonable consequence of Jose's behavior, but episodes like these tended to reinforce a negative perception of Jose on the part of his teacher and his peers.

Connecting with other outsiders can further this trend as well. For example, Pablo often sat next to Ari during whole-class gatherings. Ari, a neighborhood student, often called negative attention to himself with loud and mischievous behavior. Pablo enjoyed sitting next to Ari, who showered him with attention and included Pablo in his misadventures. Frequently, though, Georgia would interrupt the class activities to berate one or both boys, and, in this way, Pablo became identified with Ari's disruptive behaviors.

Several teachers remarked about the negative behavioral consequences of Canford students who primarily befriend either other program students or other outsiders. As Pam states, "I see how Christopher relates to the three Hispanic kids in the other rooms, to Jose and Pablo and Juan. It's just . . . it's totally different than the way he relates to kids here. Um . . . here I feel he's really, just as a peer, I don't think he thinks of himself as, I mean, he's not like trying to be somebody he isn't, but I think he wants so badly to be Jose and Pablo's friend, and he sees the two of them friends and together, and he's jealous, so he does crazy things to attract their attention and to try and get in. And

I see that on yard duty, but I don't see that kind of stuff in the classroom." Georgia also notes some of the complications of the friendship between Juan and Jose: "Juan and Jose now are big friends, which is good for them, but it's not so good for Jose. I don't know. It's good, I guess, that they have friends. It's fine outside, but inside, Jose's getting in a lot more trouble. So, it's good that they do have friends, but it's not a very productive friendship inside."

A General Cycle of Exclusion

Making friends is a fundamental element of schooling, the essence of social integration, and a key factor in school success. Perhaps there is a paradoxical tradeoff here for parents and children of the Canford Program. Canford parents choose to seek enhanced educational opportunities for their children by sending them to crosstown schools. Multiple factors, however, make it difficult for the children to succeed socially, which may in turn affect the overall success of the school experience for these students.

A conceptual model of the development of social connections for Canford students in their Arbor Town school settings demonstrates the flip side of the Great Cycle of Social Sorting, described earlier. On the one hand, this conceptual model helps to explain the strong connections Canford students build with one another: they have more shared experiences and opportunities to interact, leading to greater shared understandings and an attraction which leads to further opportunities to interact. On the other hand, in the broader context of the social setting at their school sites, the Canford students appear to be engaged in a cycle of exclusion or separation.

To begin with, Canford students have few opportunities to interact with neighborhood Arbor Town school peers outside of the school day, and they come to the setting with few, if any, social peers at the outset. This lack of proximity and mutual understanding ("propinquity" and "intersubjectivity") tends to put Canford students on the periphery of social interactions at the school site. Their relationships to Canford peers, based on a common bus-riding experience and other social and cultural considerations outside of school, have a negative impact on their opportunities to integrate with their classmates from Arbor Town. Once on the outside of the social scene, they tend to match up with other outsiders and have fewer opportunities to join in the central play with school peers. As a consequence, they often develop negative behaviors that further mark them as outsiders, lessening their capacity to fit into the central play, and so the cycle continues. In sum, these factors seem to make it more difficult for the Canford students to gain access to the tools, resources, spaces, and peers they may need to become fully participating members in this social community.

V

The Obstacle Course of Schooling

You Not S'pose to Use *That* Word *in School!*

I have been waiting at the bus stop at Shady Grove Elementary for about twenty minutes with several Canford students. The South Bay City bus is late again, so the Canford students are the last ones remaining to be picked up from school. The children are more active and louder than they typically are during the regular school day, even on the playground. My attention focuses on Holly, whom I hear singing. Her song sounds a bit like a jump rope rhyme, though not one that I recognize. I ask her about it. Jerome, a second grader in the Canford Program, is sitting next to Holly along a three-foot-high cement wall. The children, both of whom are African American, swing their feet as they dangle them above the ground.

Jerome and Holly begin explaining to me that this song is related somehow to Jerome's football games. Jerome then tells me that his team is called the Mustangs.

Holly: "Nuh-uh! Your team is the *Junior Pee Wees!*"

Jerome: "Yeah, but the team name's Mustangs."

Holly: "Don't you try to tell me none of that! It ain't no Mustangs. You the Junior Pee Wees!"

Holly persists in putting Jerome down for trying to call his team the Mustangs when she thinks they are called the Junior Pee Wees. When he tries to plead his case, she continues to harass him: "Nuh-uh! Don't you tell me that! I don't hear that! Tell it to the hand. The invisible hand!"

Holly puts her hand, palm forward, in Jerome's face. She shakes her head back and forth, rolls her eyes up in her head, and looks away. Jerome reacts by putting his hand up too.

Jerome: "Tell it to the hand! Tell it to the hand!!" he calls out loudly.

Then Jerome begins to hurl a quick string of insults at Holly. His exact phrasing is difficult to capture, but it includes both expletives and racial epithets.

Holly: "You not s'pose to use *that* word *in school!*"

Throughout this exchange, the children are engaged in linguistic and interactional patterns that I have not seen displayed during the regular school day. For example, they are both using more vernacular speech and tone, talking more rapidly, and using lots of gestures and facial expressions, all of which differ from the typical pattern I have observed in the classroom and on the school playground.

At this point, Jerome and Holly part company. A bit later, Holly and I engage in a conversation about her friends on the bus. I ask her to clarify how she knows Jerome.

Holly: "We both live in South Bay City. The white people, they call it 'South-uh Bay-uh Cit-ee.' [Holly tries to affect a "white" accent. Her inflection is higher, slower, and more monotone.] The white people, . . . they make me laugh sometimes . . . I'm *black!* I'm *very* black!"

Holly then looks down at her hands, pulls up her shirtsleeve, and indicates the dark-toned skin on her arm.

In this narrative, we see Holly in a transitional time and space. The school day has ended, and Holly is anticipating her journey back to her home community on the school bus. She is navigating her role in two very different spaces. In doing so, Holly illustrates how the Canford students need to figure out which linguistic ranges, cultural and interactional practices, and other behaviors are appropriate to different times and places during the school day. Holly's efforts are laudable and poignant, and we can learn a great deal from them.

Adapting successfully to school is much more complex than just moving between the home and school environments. By itself, this is a complicated enough venture for students who are transferring from a neighborhood situated in a far different context than the one in which their schools are located. Beyond this challenge, Canford students also have to navigate the more subtle distinctions among their multiple activity settings and transitions throughout the school day. In order to fit in and succeed, the students need to adapt and adjust to a multitude of contexts, each with its own set of expectations and norms, all of which requires a level of sophistication and flexibility difficult for many youngsters in the setting to realize.

Adapting to Multiple Venues

In a study of sixteen first graders, all recent immigrants with little or no fluency in English, Brizuela and Garcia-Sellers (1999) explore the students' relationship with their home and school environments. The authors conclude that for some students the culture of the home and that of the school converge, fostering potential benefits such as an ease of transition from one setting to the other and the availability of a host of support networks. For other students there is little, if any, overlap in the norms and expectations of these domains, creating a more difficult transition from one setting to the other and other potential difficulties as well. The authors maintain that successful school adaptation requires some confluence of expectations between home and school environments, as well as strong communication and support across the two environments. In addition, the authors advocate for a mediator between the school and home environments to support the transition process for students beyond what teachers might be able to provide on their own.

The notion of an interactive adaptation process is echoed in the work of Phelan, Davidson, and Yu (1998). In their study of adolescent students, the authors describe a similar interaction among three spheres of influence: home, school, and peers. These scholars suggest that students whose "multiple

worlds" have greater overlap in terms of norms, values, and expectations tend to adapt better to the school setting than students whose home and community lives have less in common
with the school culture. Phelan, Davidson, and Yu advocate a
proactive stance on the part of educators in terms of understanding and supporting students in managing these multiple
worlds: "As educators attempt to create optimal school environments for increasingly diverse populations, we need to
know how students negotiate boundaries successfully, or, alternatively, how they are impeded by barriers that prevent
their connection not only with institutional context, but also
with peers who are different from themselves. We believe that
understanding students' multiple worlds and boundary crossing behavior is vital in a world where barriers continue to
block understanding and obstruct attempts to develop and
implement policies to ensure the success of *all* students in
today's schools" (226).

Considering a student's multiple worlds helps illuminate
a valuable conceptual understanding of the transition and
adaptation process the Canford students (and others) must
navigate in order to achieve success in the school setting. During the course of a school day, Canford students must bridge
an incredible number of different settings or venues, each of
which has its own set of expectations, practices, and norms.
The Canford students generally have a difficult time adapting
to the Arbor Town school scene. As they struggle to adjust to
their school community, they are often found on the periphery of activity or outside of the expectations for a particular
venue. Many of the Arbor Town teachers relate difficulties
the Canford students face in making the adjustment across
boundaries, describing the general distress students endure in
traveling from their homes in South Bay City to the Arbor

Town schools. One teacher puts it like this: "I think it's a big shock once they get here. Yeah, just the cultural shock. Even at the kindergarten level. The richness of the atmosphere and all there is to do. . . . Some of them were just terrified the first couple weeks of school, they just clung to me . . . I wish it could be easier for them, because I think just being here is a big change."

A second teacher notes the difficulty that one of her students has in making this adjustment to Arbor Town from South Bay City: "I mean, when he came, he was terrified. . . . He was very frightened and he would, literally, hang onto my leg for about the first two months of school. He didn't let go of me. . . . He was frightened . . . and so it was a long road from his starting point to the person he was by the end of the year."

Yet another teacher adds: "Actually, these kids are having to live in two worlds, they really are. I mean, what they see and what they're exposed to here, some of them go back and it's like a totally, totally different experience."

Moving across boundaries and between venues is a complicated task, especially for transitioning students like those in the Canford Program whose multiple worlds have few overlapping features. As one Arbor Town district administrator put it, a successful Canford student is "one who can walk in all worlds."

A Long Day's Journey: Paloma's Odyssey

The transition between school and home is clearly difficult and complicated for Canford students. In fact, based on my research, I would suggest that the multiple worlds model, though germane, oversimplifies the complexity of this endeavor. For example, while the model treats the culture of school as a single entity, the Canford students work to adapt to dozens of localized activity venues within the school setting each day. The adaptation process in these multiple settings is extraordinarily complex and rigorous, as each venue is likely to have a particular set of understandings, practices, and expectations. Adapting to school requires mastery of each of these particular venues, rather than mastery of a unified school setting.

Paloma's daily schedule (compiled based on interviews with her teachers and her mother and my experiences shadowing her over the course of a full school day) helps highlight the complex web of venues and transitions she and the other Canford students must adapt to on a daily basis (table 5.1). All told, Paloma puts in a very full twelve-hour workday, from the bus stop at dawn to pick-up at the day care center in the evening. According to her mother, Paloma is awake by 6:00 A.M. and needs to be fed, dressed, helped to get organized for school, and delivered to the bus stop by 6:45. She is often picked up from day care as late as 6:00 P.M., leaving perhaps just enough time for evening chores and rituals including dinner, bathing, television, homework, and bedtime routines. Paloma's mother, a young, single, working parent of two children, does her best to put Paloma to bed by about 8:30 P.M. in the hopes that Paloma will have enough energy to begin the routine over again early the next morning.

Paloma's schedule illuminates the dozens of different venues and transitions she encounters on a daily basis, each with a distinct character and set of appropriate practices. Successful participation in one venue, such as riding on the bus, requires a very different set of skills and understandings than does another, such as interacting in a classroom meeting. Working on a writing task during "table time" with the classroom teacher involves different parameters than a similar

Table 5.1   Paloma's School Day

6:00 – 8:05 A.M.   Preparing for School
- 6:00   Wake up, dress, eat breakfast, prepare for the day
- 6:45   Leave home and walk to the bus stop with family
- 6:55   Board the school bus
- 8:05   Arrive at school (5 minutes late)

8:05 – 11:30 A.M.   Kindergarten Morning
- Morning transition activities
- Circle time (singing and story)
- Class meeting
- Small-group activity
- Choice time
- Cleanup
- Whole-class activity
- Lining up
- Library time
- Outdoor play
- Snack time
- Class meeting
- Table time
- Language tutoring (in class)
- Cleanup
- Closing circle

11:30 A.M. – 1:30 P.M.   Kindergarten Afternoon
- Lunch, outdoor time (different supervisors)
- Class meeting
- Science activities
- Resource specialist support (pull out)
- Return to science activities
- Cleanup
- Closing circle
- Dismissal
- Walk to bus stop

(continued)

Table 5.1   *(continued)*

1:30 – 6:00 P.M.	**After School**
1:30	Board bus to day care center
2:00	After-school program (includes a variety of large-group, small-group, and individual choice activities with different adult supervisors and peers)
6:00	Pickup from day care by mother

activity with a language tutor. The level of subtlety can be surprising. For example, story time with a classroom teacher may exact different demands on the students than story time with the librarian. Thus the adaptation process these students are expected to achieve is a highly complex and sophisticated one.

Competing Expectations Make Adaptation Difficult

I provide two examples here to help clarify why this process can be so daunting. To begin with, many of these activity venues have contradictory sets of expectations. Since many venues that students are engaged in have few or no overlapping qualities, the task for transitioning students is more complicated.

First, the bus ride to school provides a prime illustration. It is important to note that from the students' perspective, the bus ride is an educational setting—or at least a school-sanctioned one—even if it is largely ignored by school practitioners. Students can and do learn crucial lessons on the bus. Based on conversations with students about the bus rides and my own experiences riding the bus with the Canford students, I list here some of the ways students learn to fit in and succeed in this setting:

- sharing or withholding snacks from others to gain power, status, and camaraderie;
- sneaking food onto the bus in defiance of authority in order to have access to these valuable resources;
- teasing and engaging in physical play, which are accepted modes of interaction;
- employing vernacular and native language, which is valued;
- using insults and profanity, which also have their place;
- displaying aggression and using physical confrontation to solve problems among peers.

The moment these students step off the bus, they enter a completely different world with a unique set of norms, practices, and expectations. The lessons the students learned in one venue can and do get them in trouble in the next. For example, settling in for an early-morning whole-class meeting where the teacher expects students to be compliant, still, calm, and quiet often proves to be difficult for Canford students transitioning from a rowdy bus ride.

Distinctions among practices in clearly differentiated venues such as the bus and the classroom may be easily recognizable from an adult perspective, but they can prove to be a stumbling point for transitioning students. Additionally, less obvious variations on this theme occur throughout the school day, and the subtlety of these distinctions makes transitions even more difficult for the students. This effect is particularly true for the Canford students, who are frequently less comfortable and settled in the school setting from the outset.

In a second example, the kindergarten students take a
trip once a week to the school library, where they check out
and return library books and listen to a story read by the librarian. From the adult perspective, such practices may seem
routine for schoolchildren, but for transitioning students,
variations in expectations and practices can be particularly
troublesome. (I would also add that while from the perspective
of adults such activities as checking out books from the library
may seem simple, such practices must be learned at some
point, and a great deal of kindergarten students' time at school
may well be dedicated to routines that we may take for granted
as adults.) The following description of a class trip to the library is indicative of the way Canford students often emerge as
outsiders in various school settings.

> Today is Library Day for Anita's class. The students
> are all lined up by the classroom doorway, and most
> of them are carrying books under their arms to re-
> turn to the school library, having checked them out
> during last week's visit. I stand at the end of the line
> next to Tali and Marikit, the two Canford students
> in Anita's class.
>
> We walk out of the classroom and across the
> schoolyard to the library. As the children pass
> through the doorway, they file past the librarian's
> desk to return books into a wide slot at the check-
> out desk. As Marikit walks up to the book slot, she
> looks around the room for Anita. When Marikit
> spots her teacher, she holds up her library book and
> shrugs her shoulders, a quizzical look on her face.
> Anita nods her head in affirmation, and Marikit
> slides her book into the slot.

After returning their books, the students meander toward the Reading Rug. The space is a sunken area in the center of the room with a rug on the floor and two small steps leading down to it. The librarian, Ms. Carney, usually sits in a rocking chair on the lowest level.

As Anita's students enter the "Reading Rug" area, they arrange themselves on the steps. Ten of the students sit in the front row along the bottom step directly facing Ms. Carney. Six others sit behind this group on the top step, also facing the librarian. Tali takes a seat away from the group in the adjacent steps to the right of Ms. Carney, and Marikit sits on the steps to Ms. Carney's left. In this way, the two Canford students separate themselves physically from the rest of the group.

During the course of the lesson, both Tali and Marikit distinguish themselves from the rest of the group in many ways. They not only segregate themselves physically but also behave quite differently from the other students.

Tali is an active participant in the lesson, but unlike most of the other students in the group she has not picked up on Ms. Carney's expectations for story time in the library. Although Anita tends to be open to students' spontaneous thoughts and questions during classroom read-alouds—particularly those from Tali—Ms. Carney is more strict and her routines more structured. During the reading Tali frequently calls out comments about the story, and she wanders across the step, nearer to the group, as she does so. Her running commen-

tary sounds something like this, with a comment
every few seconds:

"Look at him!"

"Looky, his bathtub's muddy!"

"Funny!"

"If I jumped out of that plane, what would
happen?"

None of the other students make any comments about the story except in direct response to
Ms. Carney's questions.

At one point, Ms. Carney leans to her right
and says, "Tay-li, you need to wait until I'm finished."
Ms. Carney mispronounces her name, using a long
"a" sound instead of a short "a." Several students
call out, "It's Tali!" to correct Ms. Carney. At this
point, Tali quiets down and crawls from the lower
to the top step and back away from the group. Tali
looks intently at the book while Ms. Carney reads
on, but she makes no further comment.

Meanwhile, Marikit has slowly moved farther
away from the group toward the edge of her set of
stairs, near the wall. She rolls up and down steps on
her knees, toes, hands, and back. From time to time
she glances up at the book, but it is hard to tell if she
is engaged with the story.

At the end of the reading, Ms. Carney asks the
students a series of questions about the story,
querying who has read the book before, whether
this book is similar to or different from other books
she's read to the class, what the character in the
story might have been thinking, and so on. In response to the first few questions, Marikit raises her

hand but is not called on. After that, she stretches out on the top step and lies down on her back. At this point, Ms. Carney looks over and asks Marikit, "Can you see the pictures from there?" Marikit quickly calls out "Yeah," rolls down to the bottom step, and sits up. She yawns and looks away.

In fact, Marikit is one of the better readers in the class, yet Ms. Carney asks her only about the pictures, not the story or the words. She seems to notice Marikit not when it comes to the heart of the discussion but rather in terms of her adherence to the norms and routines of the library time. The same holds true for Tali. The content of her remarks is ignored, but her behavioral style becomes a focal point. In this way, Marikit and Tali find themselves outside of the behavioral expectations of one particular activity setting. Perhaps these students would get a chance to play a more central role either if they were able to participate more fully in the expected routines during library time, or if Ms. Carney were more open to a wider range of student behaviors. It is fair to note that while a classroom teacher and a particular student may have adjusted expectations, procedures, and interactional patterns together over time, a librarian who sees several hundred students over the course of a day might understandably demonstrate less flexibility. Such practices, however, are likely to marginalize students who already find themselves on the outside looking in.

Indeed, inflexible expectations do tend to further marginalize the Canford students, who already have difficulty sorting out routines, and they become likely to fall on the outside of the norms in an ever-broadening array of settings and venues. If the adults responsible for orchestrating learning opportunities and establishing norms in particular venues do not attend to the conditions relevant to the full range of their students, they may well be creating difficulties for those most prone to falling outside of implicit boundaries.

The Canford students' experiences after the bus ride and at the library highlight what I call the "obstacle course of schooling." Students are expected to move quickly from one event (such as the bus ride) to another (the class meeting), often with little training or preparation. Moreover, the obstacle course comes with a rulebook that seems to be rewritten at various junctures. Students often seem unsure of which set of rules is in play at a given time, and their missteps are both evident and consequential. Furthermore, the course may change from day to day or setting to setting without notice, making it even more difficult to master.

Participation in the obstacle course of schooling is not limited to the Canford students. Trouble navigating the course is common for schoolchildren, particularly for kindergarten students, who all endure an adjustment and transition to primary schooling in one way or another. Yet for students like those in the Canford Program the course is more challenging. They have to clear additional hurdles and traverse greater distances, physically, culturally, linguistically, and otherwise. Because the challenges are exaggerated for them, their experience highlights the obstacles for us.

An expansive conception of the complex web of venues the students must traverse provides, perhaps, a deeper and more realistic picture of the school adaptation process. Not only are the children endeavoring to bridge their multiple worlds—the potentially competing norms and expectations of their home community, the school community, and their peers—but each of these settings is composed of a host of overlapping and competing activity settings and fields of influence. The school setting is not a monolithic institution with one set of values, practices, expectations, and norms to discern. Mastering such a setting would be a complex task in itself, especially for students whose home community or influential peers hold different sets of expectations, valued skills, and norms. But the school setting comprises numerous activity venues—the bus, the playground, library time, circle time, recess, small group activities, free choice time, transitions, snack, and more— so the task for students is all the more complex.

Furthermore, this notion illustrates only one intricate piece of a much larger puzzle. I have emphasized school-related activity settings here. If we take this more complex picture of the school setting and overlay it with a more complex picture of the other milieus in which students must work and adapt, we can get a better sense of the truly difficult course that these students traverse each day.

Transitions: Time and Space between Activity Settings

Adapting to ever-changing expectations across multiple activity settings is difficult, and the Canford students must also contend with transitioning among these distinct activity settings, as well. In fact, the transition process may well be the most difficult part of this assignment. Transitions in time, space, and norms between venues are a key feature of the school experience. These transitions may be most obvious between the broad domains of home and school, but they are also quite evident between the classroom and the library, for example, or from a class meeting to table time activities, or from the playground back to the classroom.

Each transition provides a new opportunity for the students to demonstrate their understanding of the prevailing expectations and to settle into the center of their new environment. Several key questions emerge during these routines: Do the students know it's time for another change? Do they prepare the right tool set for the coming activity setting? Can they sort out the subtle differences in activity, energy, noise levels, and other norms? Do they get lost or follow suit?

Because the transitional times and events are typically less structured than other activities, they provide an opportunity for students to sort out expectations and express themselves in different ways than they might during more tightly scripted activity settings. Transitional moments are also less likely to be closely monitored by classroom teachers or other instructors.

So, on the one hand, significant transitional spaces, such as the bus and the bus stop, and venues with more flexible boundaries, such as the play yard or snack time, seem to provide students with an opportunity to more flexibly and comfortably express themselves. Students who are nearly silent in classroom activity settings often have their most vibrant exchanges with peers while walking in line from one place at school to another or while waiting at the bus stop. On the other hand, transitional times and places are also ones where students are apt to get lost, fall behind, and get into trouble. Because transitional events provide less structure, less oversight, and fewer clear behavioral guidelines, the children are more likely to be caught outside of shifting boundaries.

This transitional work is evident in many of the narratives I have described. Holly's work at the bus stop to transition from her "school" self to her "bus" or her "community" self as she waits for the school bus to take her home is an example of a student sorting through some of the varying expectations of different venues. Alex's and Jose's game of chase in between the bus stop and the classroom is an example of the many times when students get lost or distracted during transitions. Felix's concern about the bus rides is heightened during the transitional story time at the end of his day. Many Canford students find themselves most apt to get in trouble with their teachers and peers while waiting in line to move from one activity to another. Examples abound in my observations of scores of daily transitions.

The process of continuously shifting between venues tends to keep these students off balance, and it is often difficult for them to recover. Even when students do manage to recover their footing and get settled—say, to move from the transition at the bus drop-off to the opening routines of the classroom— the teacher often changes expectations on them again just as they get themselves sorted out. Remember, for example, Marikit's first day of school, where she just begins to engage in a drawing activity as the transitional period ends and the first class meeting begins. Over and over, I would see the Canford students as the laggers: the last in line, the last to put things away, last to a table, last to complete an assignment. These are not just indications of their developing English-language and school-readiness skills—as many teachers are apt to conclude. I believe it is an artifact of their place on the periphery of these communities to which they are trying to adjust and adapt. It is easier to accomplish these transitional feats if one is "settled" in Place A and trying to see how Place B might be different. If one is already struggling to find a rhythm in Place A, moving comfortably to Place B proves even more difficult.

Anita underscores this point in one of our interviews, noting how Canford students are more susceptible to the impact of slight adjustments: "I'm wondering if they've [Canford students] come to school not on two firm feet every day, and then when something else comes up, it knocks them over more, and they may react to it longer or more significantly. It might be a small thing to other kids or a normal thing to other kids, and it's just, like, *more* to them because of all the things like taking a long time to get here on the bus, and it's a different culture, and all of those other things." The work of transitioning between venues is another example of the complexity of the school experience endeavor for the Canford students. The obstacle course of schooling is a daunting and exhausting exercise. We would do well to recognize and appreciate the efforts students undertake in this involuntary competition, and to think about the roles we play in adding additional hurdles or providing supportive coaching.

VI
Leopards and Chameleons

In *Doing School* (2001) Denise Pope describes how academically successful adolescents navigate the educational system by sorting out the routines and procedures that will help them survive in a competitive system rather than by focusing on the purported academic and intellectual pursuits of the institution. In a similar way, the work of the Canford students to navigate the multiple venues and transitions they encounter each day can be seen as a form of "doing school." In many ways, the most successful students are the ones who sort out the particular routines, procedures, and expectations of different settings and who can differentiate among these wide-ranging sets of norms. Often, these norms and their related cues are quite subtle and difficult to discern, making this complex task even more challenging.

In the following narrative Pablo is seen having difficulty sorting out his teacher's expectations for story time, a common problem for Canford students.

Georgia has all of the students sitting around the perimeter of the rug space for the "morning meeting." The class has been sitting together for about fifteen minutes through a morning song, followed by a set of calendar activities and taking attendance. Georgia now pulls out a book, Joseph Slate's *Miss Bindergarten Gets Ready for Kindergarten* (1996), and tells the students to quiet down for the story time. The book is an alphabetic story depicting a series of characters who will be students in Miss Bindergarten's class. Each character represents an animal whose name begins with a particular letter of the alphabet, from Adam the alligator to Zach the zebra.

At the end of the story, Georgia reviews with her class the names of all the animals connected with the story's characters. One is them is an iguana. After hearing this, Pablo turns to his neighbor and says aloud, "Iguana? Iguana?" Pablo has a quizzical look as well as a grin on his face. He seems to be testing out the word, which may well be new to him. Georgia turns and looks at Pablo and says, "Pablo, shh!" and puts her finger to her mouth. She then adds, "It's okay to laugh at the story. I don't mind if you laugh, but not if you're interrupting the whole story."

Georgia maintains a subtle balance between student participation and a quiet atmosphere during her story times. While at some points she elicits and responds to comments and questions that her students express spontaneously, at other times she demands relative calm and quiet, often interrupting her own lessons with a loud "Shhh!" or a "Quiet please!" These efforts to calm the class are usually aimed at the group at large, and they generally have the effect of very briefly lowering the background chatter. At the peak of her attempts to control the din, Georgia will often sharply call out an individual student by name, narrowing her brow and directing a focused look at that student, all of which appears to connote that this student needs to better control his or her behavior. From the students' perspective, figuring out how to participate in related story discussions without being singled out for negative behavior is one form of "doing kindergarten."

Over the first several months of school, Pablo's primary tactic for surviving the complexities of the obstacle course of schooling was to hide. Not having the camouflage needed to blend into multiple environments, he chose to hide in the thicket, hoping not to get noticed. Pablo would usually sit in the back of whole-class meetings, and he would not volunteer questions or answers, often even when called upon directly.

As the school year wore on, Pablo became more emboldened in his participation in whole-class activities, but he had a difficult time sorting out the level of vocalizing that Georgia would tolerate at any given time. While many students seemed to notice, for example, that the frequency of Georgia's shushing often increased just before she called out someone's name, Pablo remained oblivious to this pattern. In fact, the louder the environment became, the more likely he was to speak up. He became more comfortable speaking out when others around him were doing so. This seems like a reasonable strategic approach, but it was not the right one for this particular setting. As a result, Pablo's name was called out more often as the school year wore on, and he became more noticeable to his teacher, and in turn his classmates, in a negative light.

Sorting out the difference between "laughing at the story" and "interrupting the whole story" is a complicated business and requires a careful study and understanding of the particular practices of the teacher or other adult in question. In this way, one of the lessons of schooling even for such young students is that one of the keys to success is sorting out what teachers want and expect. Some students come to school with a repertoire of appropriate, conforming behaviors, and others have more work to do in acquiring them. Pablo and most of his Canford peers are in the second category.

Furthermore, different venues have different expectations. Story time with the classroom teacher differs from story time with the librarian or story time with a substitute, or the language tutor, or the parent volunteer. Each of these interactions requires a different set of tools and practices to navigate smoothly. Figuring out how to "do story time" in one venue does not necessarily enable students to navigate story time successfully across school settings. All told, successful navigations demand an incredibly sophisticated understanding of how to adapt in different venues—how to "do kindergarten."

Given the difficult obstacle course these students are asked to run—bridging home, community, and school; adapting to the multiple activity venues of schooling and adjusting to their fluctuating expectations; and transitioning among these various settings—how do the Canford students fare? What are the characteristics of their response to this challenge?

In her book, Pope maintains that the work her students do to adjust and adapt to the shifting demands of various settings makes them into "classroom chameleons." Those who best manage to camouflage their behaviors in ways their different teachers find appropriate tend to be more effective in the high school setting. Similarly, the Canford students are expected to adapt and adjust to a multitude of environments, figuring out how to fit in to a wide range of contexts. I would argue that they too are expected to be chameleons of a sort, to transform their behaviors in ways that help them fit in and succeed in different venues.

At least one important distinction holds between the work of adolescents and that of primary students in this adaptive process. One of the students in Pope's study, discussing her own adaptive behaviors, says, "If you learn how to manipulate the system, then you learn how you can survive in high school without going nuts" (149). These adolescents recognize their adaptive behaviors as efforts to survive and excel within a confusing school system that offers conflicting goals. While the Canford kindergarten students face some of the same dilemmas, they are largely not conscious of the challenge set before them. In this way, the scene is complicated even further: not only are the students engaged in a complex and challenging endeavor, this obstacle course of schooling, but they are broadly unaware that they are even playing the game.

Some students seem to have a greater inclination to adjust and adapt their behaviors in the various venues than others. But by and large, the Canford students are not very successful in playing the chameleon.

The Leopards

The Canford students are more analogous, perhaps, to leopards. Their camouflage is unable to change rapidly to fit a new environment. There is a strength, grace, and beauty to the students' efforts, yet they are not well suited for or adaptable to many of the school settings in which they find themselves. While the leopards may fare well in certain situations, these students often seem to be caught in an environment in which they are lost, confused, and out of place.

Callie serves as a prime example of the leopards. Like most of the Canford students, Callie has difficulty adjusting and adapting to her teachers' wide array of procedures and expectations. Callie also frequently fails to follow the rituals set for her table group, leading her peers to pressure her toward conformity. While she has several strengths, including a love of books, an inquisitive mind, perseverance, and a penchant for storytelling, she is most often recognized by her teacher and her peers for the ways that she stands out from the group. Like a leopard, Callie has a camouflage that may serve her well in a particular environment, but it is not well suited for many others. Callie takes her spots with her from setting to setting, and she seems out of place more often than not. The following observations are just a few examples.

As she has done for each of the past several weeks, the librarian has come to Callie's classroom to do some activities with the students and to read them a book. The students are initially arranged around the classroom rug in a circle for a greeting activity with the librarian. Afterward, she asks the students to move for the story time. "Gather together like a bunch of grapes," the librarian tells the students, and they begin to congregate near her chair in a clump. "Don't forget not to squish each other. We don't want any grape juice!"

While most of the students are arranging themselves for the story, Callie has wandered away from the meeting rug to the sink, where she gets a drink of water from the fountain and lingers for a while. Once most of the students are settled, Callie comes rapidly to the very front of the clump of students, arranging herself in a tight space between two other children and directly in front of another. "Callie, you're squishing me!" Courtney calls out in a whining tone. Callie turns around, frowns, and glares directly into Courtney's face. "Callie! Stop!" Courtney complains. "Turn around please, Callie," the librarian says, and she then calls for the group's attention. All of the students, including Callie, look up and listen as the librarian begins to read the story aloud.

We can look at Callie's actions in many different ways. In one sense, she can be seen as asserting herself, working to take a seat front and center, ready to attend to the activity at hand. She loves books and stories, and she is actively working to grab a central space for the event. Yet Callie seems to manage this at the expense of her relationship and reputation with her peers and possibly with her teacher as well. Unlike the other students who have learned to "gather together like a bunch of grapes" without making any "juice," Callie follows her own path to the story time. First, without asking for permission, she takes a break to the water fountain, and then upon her return she forces her way to the front. Callie aggravates her peers and calls attention to herself this way with great frequency.

Another day, while at her table group, Callie is chatting quite actively while working on her journal. The teacher's stated expectation is that the students will work quietly during journal time, and she rewards quiet tables with points that she tallies on the chalkboard. Callie's tablemates often plead with her to be less talkative so they can acquire more table points. On one occasion, a tablemate pleads, "No talking, Callie!" to which Callie responds, "I have to talk! I'll die if I don't talk!"

I believe that Callie is expressing a notable part of herself in this exchange. She has a strong need and a gift for verbal expression, and her chatting, which is frequently related to the stories she writes in her journal, is probably useful to the work she is pursuing. At the same time, this aspect of her personality clearly puts Callie at odds with the norms and expectations in her classroom, and as a result she has ongoing difficulties with both her peers and her teacher.

Christopher is another student who has trouble sorting out or engaging in the expected behaviors in many settings. Consequently, like Callie, Christopher frequently calls attention to himself in an unflattering way, often as he tries to engage and participate in meaningful ways. The following example is illustrative:

During a whole-class gathering, Pam is showing the students a collection of shells she has brought back from a trip to the beach. Christopher is sitting at the front of the group just to Pam's left. He sits on his knees and peers closely at the shells as Pam displays them. During the activity, several students call out "Christopher!" and beseech him to "sit criss-cross!" with his legs folded in front of him, as is the expectation in Pam's class. Christopher sits down on hearing the pleas from his peers, but it appears that he can't quite control his enthusiasm for the shells, and he continues to bounce up onto his knees. Finally, as his peers call out his name louder and louder, Christopher crawls away from the group and sits by himself with his head in his lap, a frown on his face.

Moments later Pam dismisses some students to the water fountain, Christopher among them. As the students race to the line, several students call out his name: "Christopher!" I hear one student call out, "He's mean!" and others in the line echo, "Yeah, he's mean."

Because he has difficulty following the precise expectations of his teacher, Christopher stands out in the group. Again, like Callie, in many ways Christopher is trying to fit in and do the right thing. He is up front and paying attention, but he hasn't fit all the pieces together yet, and as a consequence he receives the negative attention of his peers. He is a misplaced leopard, unable to adapt to a novel environment. (In the final chapters I discuss the crucial role of the teacher in helping students like Christopher and Callie find their way, not just in pointing out that they are lost.)

Racial Identity and Student Adjustment

In observing the Canford students, I noted that a small subset of these students appeared to be grappling with their own racial or cultural identity. Perhaps as a consequence, they seem to have an even more difficult time adjusting to the school setting than do the other Canford students. The following narrative of Callie's behavior at dismissal time is a telling example.

Callie's teacher is dismissing her students at the end of the school day. She calls one table group at a time. The Blue Table is dismissed first, and the students make their way to their cubbies. Outside the classroom door a large group of parents and other caregivers awaits the children, who eagerly trundle along, dragging their many belongings behind them. Callie sits at the Red Table, one of the last to be dismissed. She sits facing the doorway and watches her classmates depart the classroom into the crowd of waiting adults. As she waits for her turn to be dismissed, Callie offers the following monologue: "Do you see my mom? ... She's not black. ... She's pink! ... She's white." Then Callie glares at one of her tablemates and says, "Don't look at me!"

Callie turns her attention back to the door, and she begins singing a rhyme about apples, clapping her hands and shaking her head and shoulders, rocking back and forth. "My dad might be pickin' me up today," she then adds.

She stands up and sits on top of the table, then climbs onto the table with her entire body. At this point, Callie's teacher dismisses the Red Table. Callie climbs off the table and walks to her cubby. She picks up her backpack, her lunchbox, and a handful of crumpled papers that lie at the bottom of her cubby. Then Callie exits the classroom door, and as she always does, she walks over to meet Sally, the teacher from her after-school day care program. Sally walks Callie and two other students to the on-site day care building.

Of the students, Callie is one of the most outwardly aware of and concerned with her racial and cultural identity.

Perhaps this is true in part because she is the only African American student in her class and one of the few at her school site. Unlike most of her kindergarten school peers, she mentions race in many settings, and she seems to be sorting out what it means to be black in a place where that is an uncommon trait. In this narrative, Callie seems to be relating her racial identity to another feature of her schooling experience that differs from most of her Arbor Town school peers. While most of her classmates are picked up by their parents at the end of the school day, Callie goes to the after-school day care program. While other students, including some neighborhood students, attend the day care program too, Callie notices that this is one more way she is not in the core group, in this case those who are picked up by their parents.

When Callie first asks the other students, "Do you see my mom?" she most likely knows that her mother is not outside waiting for her. Her daily routine is to proceed from school to the on-site day care center. Callie's query seems to be more of an expressed wish or a hope: she would like her mother to be outside waiting for her, like the parents of her classmates. Further, Callie appears to have connected this different experience to her own identity as someone who is African American, and her following remarks poignantly hint at uncertainty and confusion about what it means to be black in this particular place. Perhaps she is saying that were she pink or white, she might be able to be picked up by her mother at the end of the school day like most of her school peers.

Callie is also the student who preferred not to play with Cherise because Cherise is black. Such instances provide an unsettling commentary on Callie's developing sense of racial identity. Like Callie, a handful of other Canford students seem outwardly to be very conscious of their own racial and cultural identities. These same students often have the most difficulty adjusting and adapting to the multiple venues in the school setting. They are conscious of the fact that they are different from their school peers in significant ways, and at least at this stage in their schooling, these differences seem to make the school experience more troubling for them.[1]

Several teachers commented on the potential impact of a student's being one of only a handful of children from a particular racial or ethnic background. One teacher notes how difficult it can be for students who do not see many others like themselves: "Well, I think it [the difficult transition] had a lot to do with color. He just didn't see another single black kid in his class. He was terrified. I don't think he had ever been in an environment quite like that . . . where there are lots of children and none of them look like him." Another teacher comments on how the issue can be further complicated for students who are outwardly conscious of these differences: "But I've had kids that, I mean, the unfortunate state of fact was that they were the only black kid, . . . and they probably had not been in the company of that many white kids all together in one place. So, I mean, it's always hard if you're the only one. . . . And, he's a very cognizant child—aware of factors that maybe a lot of other children wouldn't have been aware of, but he is."

The experiences of these students raise some issues and questions worthy of further consideration. For example, what are the circumstances that lead children to ponder their racial and cultural identity? What might be the impact of beginning to address such deep and important questions at different ages and developmental levels? How might adults best support such endeavors for the most advantageous long-term outcomes? How can teachers, parents, and children in diverse schools foster in students both a strong and positive personal identity and an effective adaptive stance toward schooling?

"I Talk Español": Language Identity and Student Adjustment

Issues of linguistic identity also appear to have an impact on the students' experience and adjustment to the school setting, most noticeably among the students learning English as a second language. Several students out of those I observed seemed to struggle with dual language identity as they developed their English language skills.

Hector, for example, is a native Spanish speaker who rapidly acquired English language skills in kindergarten. However, balancing the cultivation of and an appreciation for his first language and the mastery of a second provides some challenges.

> As we wait for the bus to arrive, Hector tells me about his older cousin, Albert. Hector is very proud of Albert and speaks of him often in glowing terms. "He has thirteen!" Hector will say, noting Albert's age. On this day at the bus stop we are discussing language. I tell Hector and Alex that I am hoping to learn Spanish one day, and that perhaps they can teach me some words.
>
> "I talk English and Spanish," Hector tells me, "But Albert doesn't be your friend if you talk English. Only Spanish. I talk español."

Later that week Hector's teacher tells me that Hector has said he now likes English better than Spanish. She has been encouraging his confidence in his English-speaking capabilities, but now she is concerned that he seems to be valuing one language over the other. She is worried about the impact that learning a second language will have on Hector's native tongue and his cultural identity as well.

My conversations with Hector and his teacher highlight some of the barriers that students like Hector face. As he attempts to be successful in the school venue, he has to sort out how to balance his developing English-language skills with his native tongue. As John Baugh notes in *Out of the Mouths of Slaves* (1999), "Many young minority students value their vernacular dialects, including languages other than English. And many come to equate the acquisition of literacy with two negative characteristics: an abandonment of their native linguistic identity and an abhorrence of any behavior that could be considered 'acting White'" (34).

And Baugh further points out that "minority students . . . receive mixed signals regarding the power of language, and unless educators are sensitive to this fact, their nontraditional students will continue to suffer the consequences of an inferior education" (68).

The mother of another Spanish-speaking student, Felix, shared how this puzzlement over language preference and language development spilled into her family's home life as well:

> One of the things that I feel a little bit bad about is that I cannot help Felix as much as I'd like because I don't speak the language. I don't speak English that well. And sometimes Felix comes in and says, you know, "Why your books are in Spanish and mine are in English?" And I tell him, you know, "Later on when you are older you'll be able to help

me out. And, um, you will be able to teach me." . . .
And now Felix is, like, getting fluent, kind of, in
English. And he speaks in English to me when he
comes home from school. He's trying to tell me all
the things, but he always says that he cannot say it
in Spanish, that he cannot speak it or tell the experiences in Spanish. He needs to do it in English. So
I understand a little bit of what he's saying, but not
everything. I wish I could know a little bit more
about what he's sharing, but because of the lack of
language. . . . That's one of my concerns.[2]

I ask Felix's mother why she thinks he prefers to talk about
school in English rather than in Spanish. Might it be because
of a lack of vocabulary, a preference for practicing English, or
some other explanation? She replies,

Well, mhmm. I don't think it's the vocabulary.
Maybe it's a little bit difficult for him to translate
some things or to switch from one language to the
other. English is a new thing for him. And, and he's
daily using it. And then coming home and speaking
Spanish and switching, and that is a little bit hard,
so he cannot, kind of, find all the words that he
would want. When he's not talking about school he
usually uses Spanish, but when he doesn't find
the word, the real word in Spanish, he switches to
English, and also when he's talking to the baby, to
his baby brother, he's saying everything in English.

In ways somewhat similar to the racial identity issues
faced by Callie and others, linguistic identity and practices also

complicate the lives and school experiences of the Canford students.

Flexibility: Trademark of the Part-Time Chameleons

MY SCHOOL

by Paloma

My friends were playing with me on the play structure, and we all went across the monkey bars. Then we all could skip a bar, but we really can't. I could skip a bar. And then we ran into the garden and we caught roly-polies, and then we played house in the little wooden house. Then Sally was the mom. I was the little sister, and then Lisa was the baby. Sara was the big sister. And then we all played together. Then we climbed a tree, all four of us. And then Anita was watching the class, all twenty of us. All four of us saw a rainbow. The end.

Paloma's story demonstrates her approach to and place in school. She is reasonably comfortable in a number of settings and with working with others, both peers and adults. Paloma describes how she engages with her peers with some success, and the positive tenor of her story reflects her attitude and approach toward school. She displays some of the qualities of a classroom chameleon. The following narrative highlights one of Paloma's many successful interactions with her peers in the playhouse or dramatic play area.

Stacey and Alexandra, two neighborhood students, are playing together in the playhouse area. Paloma walks over to the playhouse too. She stops briefly and looks on as the girls play. Then she enters the playhouse and picks up a plastic piece of corn from the table.

"What dis?" Paloma asks.

"We're playin' farm," Stacey replies.

"I playing too," Paloma says. "I can be da cat?"

"Sure," Stacey responds, "you can be the kitty." And with this Paloma joins the girls in their farm play.

Paloma has some of the tools and skills necessary for involving herself in this play scene. Rather than directly interrupting the play, she first gravitates toward one of the artifacts of the setting. Then she engages the girls by asking about the tool, opening up an avenue for being included in the activity. Paloma is often included in the make-believe play of her peers. This is one of the areas in which she is most comfortably integrated in her classroom. Moreover, she is eventually given a key role as the "mommy" in the story.

Later on the girls decide that they want to do some writing in the playhouse. Paloma volunteers to provide some of the necessary tools. "I go ask Anita," she offers.

"Yeah! Yeah!" Alexandra and Stacey chant, and as Paloma begins to leave the scene, Alexandra calls after her, "Paloma! Paloma, get some pencils!" Paloma retrieves the supplies and returns to a heroine's welcome in the playhouse. During their celebration the girls tip over some of the playhouse furniture they've been using. "Stacey, help!" Paloma calls out as she points to the chairs. Stacey and Paloma work together to fix the scene, and then the girls all sit down and begin writing with the colored pencils and paper that Paloma has provided.

"Are you gonna be the mom?" Stacey asks Paloma.

"Yeah. I'm coloring," Paloma responds.

Here Paloma has quietly asserted herself as a leader in this play area. She has provided some useful tools to the group and has been rewarded with a key role in the play. Paloma displays some characteristics of a chameleon in her work in the playhouse. She adjusts and adapts her behaviors in ways that provide for a successful engagement.

At the same time, like the rest of her Canford peers, Paloma is unable to settle comfortably into the full range of venues in the school setting. While Paloma does have more success than most of her Canford peers in several settings, particularly in social and dramatic play opportunities with her classmates, she has difficulty in other venues. Consequently, I would characterize her as a part-time chameleon. For example, Paloma is often uncertain about the proper norms and rituals during whole-class activities, and she often chooses to follow her own path rather than acknowledge the preferences of her teachers.

The class is working with the art teacher on a mask project focused on symmetry. Paloma uses the available materials to fashion a product completely different from the one modeled by the art teacher. At the end of the lesson, the teacher asks students to show their work to the group. Paloma holds up her picture and calls out, "Look what I do!" The art teacher responds by saying, "Well, it's not symmetrical."

Most of the other students seem to be aware that the art teacher is product oriented rather than process oriented: she likes her students to follow a pattern she sets at the beginning of the lesson. Paloma is unable or unwilling to meet these expectations. Her independence and her willingness to follow her own creative spirit are commendable; still, in failing to conform to the prevailing set of norms, Paloma sets herself up to be recognized as an outsider, which has potential implications for her future success in school.

Like Paloma, most of the Canford students have moments of successful adaptation, but none of them are able to adapt consistently. Each is recognizable as an outsider or a student having difficulty in some form or another. At best they could be described as part-time chameleons.

Interestingly, Paloma appears to be unselfconscious and comfortable in pursuing her own agenda, often in spite of the prevailing rules. She is developmentally immature in various ways compared with her peers, and perhaps this lack of self-awareness contributes to her ability to fit in better than students such as Callie and Christopher. Paloma never appears to be concerned that she is different from her classmates in particular ways. She typically just pursues her own interests, with mixed results.

Style Shifting: Flexible Language Usage
and Other Transformations

The Canford kids shed their skins and put on
their armor as they get on and off the bus.
—Arbor Town teacher

Linguists describe a phenomenon whereby speakers of a nonstandard form of a dialect often exhibit a range of linguistic variation from the standard to the vernacular, applying different linguistic practices in differing contexts. Some speakers exhibit a broader and more flexible range of linguistic variation or "style shifting" than others.[3] This phenomenon is evident in my work with the Canford students, as exhibited by Holly at the bus stop, for example (see chapter 5). Along with dialectical variations among nonstandard English speakers, English language learners also exhibit variations in language practices.

Such style shifting is another way the Canford students adjust to the multiple activity venues within the school setting. The students seem to be sorting out which places are best for which linguistic styles and behaviors. All but one of the students I followed was either learning English as a second language or used a nonstandard dialect outside of school, and linguistic style shifting is a common and important practice for these students.

Language shifts are particularly apparent at transitional times and spaces. The native Spanish-speaking students principally speak English in the classroom setting. (It is also important to note that several of the language learners tended to be very quiet, or even silent, in the formal classroom setting for much of the year.) Yet, at the bus stop, on the playground, and in moving from one location to another, these students will often switch back and forth between Spanish and English and engage with one another more actively. The farther a setting is removed from the classroom, or the less structure and adult supervision are present, the more Spanish is spoken. The students speak much more Spanish on the bus than they do on the playground or while waiting in line, and they speak Spanish least often of all in the classroom.

I also observed that style shifting extends to features beyond the linguistic characteristics of the students. Students exhibit flexibility in their style of dress and the form of their interactions at various locations and with different groups of people throughout the day. Here are a few examples of this type of transformation, again demonstrating the Canford students' efforts to adapt and adjust to shifting boundaries and expectations across settings.

- At the bus stop outside the school, I see Pat, a second-grade Canford student, waiting for the bus with the kindergartners. When he first arrives at the bus stop, Pat is wearing a two-button, short-sleeved golf shirt and a New York Yankees baseball hat. His look is decidedly conventional for the college-town community of his Arbor Town school. As he waits for the bus, though, Pat changes his uniform. First, he takes his shirt off and ties it around his head like a scarf or a cap. The bulk of the shirt hangs down from his head and down his back. He then puts his baseball cap back on his head, on top of the shirt, with the brim in the back. In a matter of moments, Pat has creatively effected a completely new look, using the very same apparel.

- Jerome often wears his baggy pants in a low-riding fashion, with his underwear pulled up high and visible. This mode of dress is uncommon for elementary students in Arbor Town schools. Jerome, in fact, is the only student I observed who exhibits this style of dress, perhaps chosen as an expression of attachment to his home community, where his older brother serves as Jerome's mentor and role model in many ways, including fashion and style. Jerome often exaggerates this style of dress at the afternoon bus stop, pulling his pants down lower and his underpants higher, making his fashion statement much more pronounced as he prepares to return home. While he clearly chooses to make this statement at school, he also tones it down for the Arbor Town setting. The shift at the bus stop makes for a subtle but apparently purposeful style variation.

- Jose, Pablo, and Christopher, three of the Hispanic students in the program, typically exhibit their most aggressive physical behaviors when playing together as a group. In addition to the games of "bus tag" they play with one another during their long commutes, they play games of chase on the playground that include threatening posturing, such as raising fists in each other's faces and using menacing scowls, and that often evolve into physically grabbing and pushing one another. When working solely with one another, the boys can usually switch seamlessly between their aggressive play and friendly behaviors. It seems a comfortable routine for them. The issue becomes complicated, however, when they either involve neighborhood peers in this type of play or when they carry features of this play into other settings. An inability to sort out when such practices will be successful often leads these three boys into difficulty with peers and teachers at school.

Some of the Canford students seem to be more comfortable and proficient in these flexible performances than others. Holly, for example, is comfortable interacting in a familiar way with Jerome at the bus stop, yet when playing with her classmates on the playground she exhibits a very different linguistic and interactional style. She, more than most of the Canford students, has an understanding of the subtleties of behavior required for success in different venues. Holly's comment to Jerome in response to his use of a racial epithet at the bus stop—"you not s'pose to use *that* word *in school!*"—reflects her understanding of some of the subtle distinctions of appropriate language use and behavior in different venues. As one who can sort through various ways of being in different spaces, Holly is more successful in playing the chameleon than most of her Canford peers. Jose, Pablo, and Christopher, in contrast, have a much more difficult time knowing when, where, and with whom certain behaviors and practices are appropriate.

Navigating the multiple venues and transitions they encounter each day and sorting out the specific routines and expectations of different settings and teachers—"doing school"—is a key part of the work that the Canford students engage in on a daily basis. The part-time chameleons, those few who can figure out a way to move with some success within the complex web of venues in the school setting, tend to fare somewhat better than their peers. The leopards, on the other hand, often find that their own strengths and instincts are ill suited for the tasks and expectations at hand. As a result they are often left exposed in a precarious school environment.

VII
The Grown-Ups

While the focus of this work is on the students in the Canford Program, the adults in their lives certainly play a significant role in the story. The perceptions and decision making of the parents who choose to enroll their children in the Canford Program, the attitudes of the administrators who help to execute the program, and the perspectives and practices of the classroom teachers all have an influence on the students' experiences.

"It's Just Better!": Parents Pave the Way

The most significant decision-making adults in the lives of the Canford students are likely their parents. They are the ones who make the initial consequential decision to enroll these children in the Canford Program, choosing to opt out of the South Bay City school system and into Arbor Town.[1]

Why do these parents choose to enroll their children in the Canford Program? What drives the decision-making process? How do they learn about the Canford Program, and how much do they know about it? What motivates some parents to put their children on a long and arduous bus ride across town so they can attend schools outside their own neighborhood?

In my conversations with the parents of the Canford students, the answers to these questions were simple and consistent. All the parents with whom I spoke believed that Arbor Town's schools were vastly superior to those in South Bay City. The following comments are representative of this widely held perspective:

> It's amazing, the difference in the two school districts. It's just . . . it's just better [in Arbor Town]! I mean, you just go across a little bridge and the difference is . . . it's tremendous. . . . It's amazing, the difference!

> Yes, good schools! Anything in Arbor Town is good! I've just got to say that! Yeah, it's a better education. . . . I attended these schools here [in South Bay City], and I'm sure they haven't progressed in any way.

In addition to a general feeling among parents about the superiority of the Arbor Town schools, there was also a great deal of disdain for the South Bay City schools. The strength of parents' viewpoints is evident in comments such as these:

> I think any parent that lives in the South Bay City School District wants their kid somewhere else, period.

You know, South Bay City School District is horrible! No matter who lives there, no matter what
their ethnicity is, no matter what your background
is. That school district is horrible! And anyone
would be happy to move out.

I think Arbor Town District has more interest in the
child's future than South Bay City. I don't know,
like I said, I can't see these schools, you know. I'm
sure there's good teachers, but I've seen more of a
babysitting-type school. They're not really ... I
don't think they show much interest in the children
like they do over there. Just like I said, just the fact
that it's Arbor Town and it's a middle- and upper-
class place, I know they want the best for their kids,
so I know that's the right area for my child to be in.
It's automatic.

Parents frequently spoke in broad and general terms
about the promise of the Arbor Town schools and their impression of the clear superiority of those schools to the ones in
South Bay City. Such perceptions were deeply held. Yet very
few parents spoke to particular concerns they had with the
South Bay City schools or particular strengths of those in
Arbor Town.

Although most of the parents' comments fit into very
broad characterizations of the school systems, a few of their remarks relayed specific concerns about the South Bay City
schools. One parent, for example, shared concerns about
safety: "Well, I just don't want her going to the schools here, on
this side. I'm afraid of them. I think [Arbor Town] is safer."
And another shared a story she had heard about the lack of re-

sources in South Bay City schools: "I have friends who have children gone through the South Bay City School District, and there was one year that they didn't have enough math books for the kids to take home, so they had to like rotate days where kids could take the math book home, and then they would photocopy pages, and it was just horrible!"

One of the few comparisons mentioned by more than one set of parents was the vast difference in standardized test scores between the two school districts.[2] Several parents noted South Bay City's poor performance on California's standardized achievement tests and state Academic Performance Index rankings, especially as compared with Arbor Town schools, which generally score at or near the top of the state rankings:

> Like I said, I know their education [in Arbor Town] is hot. It ranks from nine to ten, and that's good enough for me! It's a great thing for us and a good future for my sons, I think. So I'm happy.

> Those scores [for South Bay City schools] are very low. I've seen the results in the Internet. I have a cousin of mine, he brought me information of this district, and it's the worst. It scores very low, and so I was happy to get into Arbor Town. I was already thinking about that, and I didn't want to risk my son going to these schools. So Arbor Town, to be in Arbor Town with the middle- and upper-class kids . . . I figured it was a better chance for him.

Parents' comments on their own city's schools were rather critical and harsh, and some political context may help to explain some of these negative perceptions. Shortly before and

during my study, the leading regional newspaper had run numerous stories about the South Bay City Elementary School
District focused on low test scores, troubled teachers and administrators, lawsuits against the district, and allegations of
mismanagement. The district was facing the possibility of a
takeover by the state board of education, it was the subject of
several lawsuits, and its superintendent faced charges of financial impropriety. While there may well have been significant
positive practices conducted by South Bay City teachers and
staff, the disposition of the community toward the district was
decidedly negative.

So, perhaps understandably, these parents seem to view
their decision as simple and straightforward. They believe that
they have a choice to send their children to a clearly superior
school district, and they opt to do so. The American ideal of
enhanced opportunity through educational advancement is
pervasive among these parents, and sending their children to
what are perceived as better schools is an obviously prudent
and desirable choice for them. As one district administrator
notes, "They just want the best for their kids, and somebody
has told them that this is the best thing, or somehow they've
gotten the impression that this is the best. Their neighbor or
family member told them about the program. Arbor Town has
a reputation. . . . They hear things through the grapevine and
those kinds of things."

The parents' decisions seemed to be based on general
perceptions rather than a balancing of multiple specific factors. Parents talking about the choice to send their children to
Arbor Town schools only infrequently mentioned issues such
as diversity and integration, social and emotional engagement,
extracurricular opportunities, teaching quality, curricular programs, scheduling complications, family or community pres-

sures, or other potential factors on either side of the scale. When asked about concerns or possible drawbacks to the decision, only one parent expressed any reservations, and that was over the lengthy bus ride. The parents presented a very basic rationale for their choices. Such gross comparisons may make it less likely that parents, once accepted to the program, will be active and discerning consumers of their children's educational experiences, working to spot deficiencies and effect change. This point is made by one of the Arbor Town administrators: "The parents look at it like this: well, they are doing better here than they would have been in their own district. You know, just because of the resources that are available to them. So, you're not probably going to get much argument from the parents because they feel that, you know, the kids are being given a better opportunity. And that they probably are being more successful. They are learning more. As a South Bay City parent you've just got to be happy about just being here." Underscoring this point, one parent relates how proud she is just to have moved her child out of what she considered to be a troubled district and into one she felt was vastly superior: "I am very, very satisfied about the program. It is like a dream come true for me. And, um, I feel that I have accomplished a lot. A lot of things that people—other people—have not accomplished because they probably throw the papers in the garbage. But I was able to do this, and it makes a big difference."

The parents, painting their decisions with a broad brush, are somewhat less likely to be actively engaged in the subtle dynamics and features of the school experiences of their children. If the scale they are using to measure their choices is graded only to the nearest ton, they are not likely to be concerned about pounds and ounces, though when added together those weights can make quite a difference.

Even though the parents may not be making an intricately considered choice, it is an active one. The process of enrolling in the Canford Program is not simple. Parents need to fill out paperwork in a timely manner, attend informational meetings, and follow through with school district procedures. These are parents who are clearly committed to, motivated about, and actively participating in the educational experiences of their children. This point is particularly relevant in light of some of the Arbor Town teachers' comments regarding parental support and school participation. Canford parents are often not as actively and directly involved at the school site as their Arbor Town counterparts, and some teachers read this fact as an indication that the parents are disinterested in their children's education. This stereotype is disproved by the process through which the parents enrolled their children in the Canford Program in the first place.

Administrators' Perspectives: Opening the Gates

How the Arbor Town administrators view the program is important as well. Their general approach is to view the Canford Program as limited to one of admission. The following perspective of a current administrator is telling: "First of all, we're not implementing [a set of specific activities for the Canford students]. This has been going on since 1987, so there's no implementing. . . . I think the most important thing is what [another district administrator] used to say to the parents—that the minute that they've been accepted to the Arbor Town School District and gotten through the process of the Canford Transfer Program, which is a big process, the boundaries of the Arbor Town School District extend to include their home, so they become a student with all of the rights, privileges, and services that go with that, and so the district's strategic plan involves them and folds them right into that whole thing."

In this sense, the district views the Canford students as it would any other student. In some ways this approach might be viewed as rational, and, as more than one administrator reminded me, it follows the letter of the initial agreement among the parties in the Canford lawsuit. The district has a strong track record of overall success, and it opens its doors to these additional students by fully including them in its programs and policies once their transfers are accepted by the district. I term this approach an open-door policy. From the district's perspective, its schools and programs offer a great opportunity to students, and those resources are available to the Canford students to make what they will of them.

The assumption that educational strategies that work successfully with one group of students will be equally effective with another is a precarious one, especially when the two groups may be different in significant ways. Such an approach does little to deal with the hurdles the Canford students face in the transfer process and may actually make it less likely that those challenges will be addressed. The district and program staff do find ways to support the Canford students and their families, although the teachers in my study were apt to discount or criticize most of these efforts.[3] The point here is that the perspective on this program exhibited by district administrators makes it less likely that a comprehensive approach might be taken toward the issues and hurdles faced by Canford Program students. The lack of an ongoing, comprehensive analysis or assessment of the program and the progress of its participants makes such an approach more difficult as well. One district administrator's comments highlight the unlikely prospects for meaningful assessment: "Well, there's nothing in the court order to talk about how things are going. I actually look at the situation kid by kid. But there is no way to really look programmatically. There was no mandate that we had to improve anything, and since we take the kids from kindergarten, we are working with them as they come, not taking them, say, in fourth grade, and see if we can improve their scores. So there isn't any way for me to say, really, how are things going other than: Do they get on the bus, or is the bus service there? Did they get assigned to the schools where they get registered? And all of that seems to go very well."

Teachers' Perceptions of the Canford Program

Interestingly, several of the teachers who participated in this study knew little about the Canford Program:

> When I got here, I just found out I was getting Canford kids, and I didn't even know what that meant—some disease or something [laughs]! You know, I had no idea what they were talking about.

> I don't really know too much about it. I mean, I know that they're from South Bay City and they're bused here. I don't really know why.

> I've never received any information besides they take the bus. I know it's important to know who the Canford students are for transportation purposes [laughs]. You know, like, knowing that so and so has to get on a bus, but that's basically been my correlation with Canford: okay, this student needs to take the bus.

The general impression I gathered of the teachers' under-standing of the Canford Program is that they realize they may have a small number of students in their class that typically ride the bus and reside in South Bay City. Beyond that, they are relatively uninformed about the program or its participants. More important, most teachers feel unprepared for and un-supported in working with the students in the Canford Pro-gram, decreasing the prospect of these students' receiving all of the support required to best meet their needs. As one kinder-garten teacher said, "How many teachers are prepared for hav-ing a Canford kid [laughs]? None. We have no preparation. Um ... now [the program's first coordinator] used to do a little bit, but it wasn't required. It was an after-school thing, a one-time workshop on different styles of learning. That was really good, and it was for the whole district, I think maybe a hundred people showed up. Which is good, but it wasn't enough. But it was really good, and it was somebody who talked the talk, you know, it wasn't, like a white person [laughs] saying this, it was somebody who was out in the community. So, um, everything I've learned has been because either going to, like, that one workshop or learning on my feet."

The Arbor Town teachers displayed a variety of ap-proaches to working with the Canford students in their class-rooms. Their points of view fit broadly into three categories, as described here.

"COLOR DOESN'T MATTER HERE."

Most of the teachers with whom I worked expressed a vision of teaching that espoused approaching all children in the same manner, a so-called color-blind strategy. This sentiment was related as follows by three of the teachers:

Sometimes I don't like having the background information about some of the kids, like, you know, I don't know if that's a weakness or if that's a strength, but I don't want to be . . . I just try to take them as they are and kind of assess who they are or who they are to me. And I kind of go with that. So, in terms of Canford, I'm just, I kind of don't really think about that angle or part of it.

I don't know. I just think any kid, I hope that any one of my kids would have had a great year. Like I've tried not to, "Let me do this for the Canford kids," you know? I just hope that all of them, just the way my curriculum is and the way I am, I would hope that they all had a good year.

Well, on one hand, just to kind of backtrack a little bit, like, I'm trying not to put any . . . like, I know that you're here to study the Canford students and you're more concentrated on the Canford students. I'm trying . . . I've always tried to just have them be just another child in the class.

Although there is perhaps an intuitive appeal to the logic that particular children should not be singled out for special attention or treatment, such an approach discounts or neglects the specific needs or issues that may accompany students engaged in the complex endeavor of adjusting to a novel school setting. Additionally, while many teachers proclaimed a stance of equality, in practice they often distinguished and addressed particular needs of different students in their classroom, such as special-education students or students dealing with difficulties in their personal lives like a family death or divorce. This proclaimed stance of color blindness may help teachers un-consciously shield themselves from a more in-depth consider-ation of the needs of students from different backgrounds, such as those in the Canford Program.[4]

On a few occasions the teachers' naïveté toward the in-tensity of the Canford students' experience was especially evi-dent. The following narrative highlights one such instance:

> Today Jesse's teacher, Cathy, stops me to share a story about Jesse. Jesse has been having difficulty with his behavior in class for several days, behavior Cathy describes as "defiant." He was interrupting his peers during the Table Group time, for example, and he was generally not following directions. After a conversation with Jesse, Cathy had decided to call his mother to discuss Jesse's behavior. During the course of that discussion, Jesse's mother mentioned to Cathy that Jesse had been having difficulties making friends at school and that, furthermore, one of the other students had said to Jesse, "Kids don't like you because you are black." Cathy reas-sured Jesse's mother that such behavior was un-likely to happen at school and would not be toler-ated in any event.
>
> Cathy shares with me that she does not be-lieve that this story could be true. "Color doesn't matter here," she tells me. She further relates that just before this incident, she had given an entire week's worth of lessons on Martin Luther King, Jr., and the struggles of the civil rights movement, in honor of Martin Luther King Jr. Day. She and her

class discussed how unfair and difficult things had been for African Americans in the past, and how they had improved since. She seems agitated by the situation, a feeling she reiterates in a later interview: "Yeah, I mean, I guess that's probably my biggest frustration, because I can't even tell you how many times I've said and tried to emphasize how we're all different, and we're all special. And we talked about skin color. We talked about, you know, Leo the Late Bloomer, who takes a little bit longer to write or draw or color. Like, and again and again, and I don't know why it doesn't, you know, I haven't heard . . . I never heard any racial slurs. These kids don't know that terminology."

In this instance, Cathy fails to understand the potentially problematic nature of these exchanges among the students from the perspective of Jesse or his mother. It is plausible that Cathy's students, after a week's worth of eye-opening stories about people who treated others appallingly based on their race, were identifying and remarking on salient issues of race among themselves. Moreover, can it really be surprising that Jesse, as the only African American child in Cathy's classroom, may have felt the impact of these comments particularly strongly? There is, of course, no way to know precisely what transpired among the children, and it is also quite possible that whatever happened was imprecisely interpreted by the six-year-olds involved. Still, given this confluence of circumstances, it seems reasonable to presume that some race-related incident may well have occurred. Cathy's reluctance to accept that possibility reveals an unwavering dedication to her color-blind philosophy, and at the same time it highlights some of the shortcomings of that approach. Without an acknowledgment of the particular circumstances the Canford students, and others like them, may face, educators will have difficulty dealing with such issues in an effective manner.

"I WANT THOSE CHILDREN HERE."

A smaller group of teachers had a more engaged and inquisitive approach to working with the Canford students. Tammy serves as a primary example of this group of teachers:

> Wouldn't it be great to have teachers talking to teachers who enjoy having the Canford students? You know, there are some of us. You know, all of a sudden I was thinking like, it's not always the Canford kids. They aren't always at the bottom of the barrel academically. Last year, they were my top kids. Um, but I think a lot of teachers assume there's going to be some kind of problem, and I was thinking, well, if they weren't there, then your whole class would be skewed. It would be weird, and you'd just have all these kids who were all kinda middle class. And I can't even imagine [laughs] having a class like that. It wouldn't be very real. They bring this reality, you know? We're in this little weird world over here [laughs]. And, you know, it helps us, you know, it hones teachers' ... um ... teaching skills. If we had all one kind of kid, you know, when we leave the district we wouldn't have grown so much. So, you know, a teacher could look at it in a very selfish way, that it helps them grow.

Tammy took a keen interest in the home lives and cultural backgrounds of all of her students, but particularly those from South Bay City. She went out of her way to talk with the students and their parents about their various cultural traditions and practices and encouraged them to bring some of their home lives into the classroom. Moreover, Tammy often arranged to connect with Canford families outside of school hours, spending weekends at the gardening center with one family, for example. Tammy affirmed,

> I think, to the extent that I can feel that I'm successful as a teacher, would have something to do with the sense of confidence that I had that those families were getting all the possible services they can get. I want those children here. I want those children in my class, and I want them and the parents to be getting all the support they need so that they understand what environment it is that their child is going off to basically every day, what kind of pressures their child is going off to and facing every day. So that they have enough support to understand how to help their child when it comes, for instance, to making sure that their child sits down and does homework each night because that's what they have to do. So, you know, just for the parents to really have somebody working with them, just staying with them kind of on the realities of what a child is, you know, being, you know, the pressures that their child is experiencing being here. That would be a way for me to be able to have a feeling for whether or not this was working or not working.

For Tammy and teachers like her, working successfully with the Canford students in their classrooms entailed additional effort on their part, but they were happy to make that effort.

At the same time, as John Baugh (1999) notes in a discussion of the relationships among teachers, parents, and education, such involved efforts may be difficult to cultivate and sustain: "The cooperation of parents and teachers is essential to successful education. . . . Those teachers who make the effort to contact parents—on their own initiative—tend to be far more successful with their students than those who do not. This type of extraordinary professional devotion can be taxing on teachers, however, because it is often time-consuming, unrewarded, and unappreciated" (92). In the absence of a unified approach to supporting the Canford students, the efforts of teachers like Tammy are subject to Baugh's misgivings. In my observations, such efforts, though perhaps significant and meaningful on an individual basis, were never organized or shared with others in a comprehensive manner either at the school or district level.

"The Canford Students Are the Most Difficult to Teach"

Various teachers, administrators, and other district personnel described an attitude toward the Canford students held by a third group of teachers. There was a strong sense among local educators that some of the teachers in the Arbor Town schools had a clearly negative attitude and approach to working with Canford students. As one former Arbor Town teacher told me, "You know, the Canford students are the most difficult to teach!"

Though none of the teachers in whose classrooms I conducted this study fit into this group, they expressed concerns about the views some of their colleagues held toward the Canford students. As one teacher put it, "I think there is, like, a sense with some staff, like, 'Oh, you have that many Canford kids! Oh, poor you!' You know, kind of like, it makes work harder if you have more Canfords, and 'Oh, the behavior!' and stuff. I think they're stereotyped a lot. And that puts them already in the mind that this is going to be a hard year, but I don't see it as any. . . . They're all just kids." And another stated, "Some teachers think, like, 'Oh, they're a handful!' or, 'Oh, they're going to have low scores,' or, 'There's no parent support. The parents won't give you any support.' Just stereotypes and generalizations that aren't true, but they may have had one like that and they group them all together."

No clear boundaries exist between the three categories of teachers' views. In fact, teachers often displayed complex and even contradictory approaches to their students. For example, the remarks of one teacher can be seen as approaching a stereotype, yet this same teacher often went out of her way to connect with the Canford students and their families outside of school: "I think you do definitely put in extra time. . . . Not to generalize, but I think a lot of Canford kids are extra-time kids, and everyone has different experiences, and all kids . . . I mean, I'm not saying other kids can't be, you know, extra-time kids, or other kids aren't going to do their homework, or other kids . . . but I think socially too. . . . There's something that I've seen where some of the kids don't seem to like click with a lot of other kids, and it just depends."

Different teaching stances have different implications for the school experiences of the Canford students, and the impact of stereotypes and low expectations can be devastating. Addressing the subtle and multifaceted issues of attitudes, perspectives, and prejudices—whether programmatic, racial, cultural, or otherwise—is an area worthy of further consideration, and one that demands additional time and attention on the part of program and district officials, here and elsewhere. During the course of my investigation, school and district administrators in Arbor Town offered no organized opportunities for teachers to engage in direct discussions about the Canford Program specifically or their attitudes toward or effectiveness with diverse students more generally.

The Boy Called "No!": Teacher as Perceptual Leader

The perspectives, attitudes, and approaches of teachers all have multiple implications for their students. In addition, teachers influence students' perceptions of and behavior toward their peers. The following narrative reveals one such example:

> The first thing I notice about Eduardo is the broad, bright grin on his face. His smiles are contagious. Eduardo is also quite curious. Everything he engages with in school seems new to him. He loves to explore the materials and projects available to the students. He also loves to look at books one-on-one with an adult or a peer, point inquisitively at the pictures, and make comments in Spanish or broken English. Eduardo is an energetic young boy, always on the move. Loud, vibrant, and active, he has a small, thin frame but a wealth of energy that bubbles up out of him, often in seemingly uncontrollable waves.

From my perspective as a former teacher, Eduardo appears likely to pose some challenges for his teacher. He does not quickly adapt to classroom routines and his teacher's expectations. In fact, during his first days at school, he frequently struggles to fit in. For example, when students line up at the door or are called to the rug, Eduardo often runs over to his cubby and plays with the toys in his backpack. He often spills supplies from his activity table. An avid block builder, he creates tall structures and then knocks them down, producing a loud crash and a huge mess. Additionally, Eduardo initially demonstrates very little knowledge or comprehension of English, and he begins the year with no friends at school. Like most of the Canford students, Eduardo comes to Arbor Town as something of an outsider.

During the first several weeks of school, Eduardo finds himself in conflict with the expectations of his teacher, Perry, on numerous occasions. He calls out during the story times. He pushes his way into the middle of the line. He knocks the basket of pens off of his desk. After a few days of attempting to talk through her standards and rules with Eduardo, Perry falls back on a similar refrain that she repeats after each of his missteps. "No! Eduardo!" she calls out firmly, and she then tries to set him on the right course.

The other students in the classroom quickly pick up this refrain. The phrase "No! Eduardo!" becomes one of the most repeated expressions in the classroom. The tone suggests something like what you might hear from a pet owner in the park as one dog chases another: "No, Spot! Bad dog!" In a way this phrase is applied commonly enough to become a label. Eduardo has become "No! Eduardo!" In the eyes of his classmates, he is transformed into the Boy Called "No!"

Eduardo's classmates begin to direct this phrase toward him throughout the day. For example, one day Eduardo is in line to get a drink of water from the fountain. After taking his turn he returns to the line for another sip. The cries of "No! Eduardo!" from several students are nearly instantaneous. On another day, Eduardo is walking the roll book to the office with Matthew. Along the way, rather than taking a direct route to the office, Eduardo circles in and out of the picnic tables that line the walkway. "No! Eduardo! No! Eduardo!" Matthew exclaims. On the way back, Eduardo wanders past the play structure and kicks his shoes through the sand. As he does so, Matthew frequently calls out "No! Eduardo! No! Eduardo! No! Eduardo!" When the boys return to the classroom, I am several paces behind them as they cross the doorway, but like clockwork, the first words I hear from Perry are "No! Eduardo!"

Following Perry's lead, Eduardo's classmates come to expect him to fall out of line, and they spend a great deal of time trying to catch him doing so. In an especially direct example, Olivia, one of Eduardo's tablemates, scrutinizes his actions during journal time:

The students are at their worktables, writing in their journals. Perry has asked them to draw a picture and then work on writing a description or story below their illustration. The paper has lines at the bottom for the students' writing. Eduardo is coloring very actively on the page. He has made a picture of a small house and perhaps an airplane above it, but he is now scribbling across the page in a tempestuous manner. "Oh no! Look at Eduardo! He's doing the wrong thing! Look at Eduardo! No! Eduardo! No!" Olivia points out to her peers at the table that Eduardo is coloring all over his page, not just at the top. Eventually Perry comes over to address the commotion, and after briefly reminding Olivia to focus on her own writing, Perry sits down to work with Eduardo. Perry tries to get Eduardo to confine the illustration to the top of the page while asking him about the story that might go along with his picture.

The students are thus engaged in monitoring their peer, in this case particularly because of the modeling of their teacher. They all come to expect Eduardo to engage in behaviors that require a "No!" in front of his name. Like Eduardo, many of the other Canford students find themselves on the outside of behavioral expectations, and the reactions of their teachers and peers tell them something about themselves, the educational setting, and their own role within the classroom. Through her reactions, Perry has, perhaps inadvertently, helped to push Eduardo further from the center of her own classroom community. By labeling him "No! Eduardo!" she assigns him a place and role outside of the center, and she makes this status clear not only to Eduardo but also to his classmates and the other adults in the room. From that distance, Eduardo will likely find it even more difficult to find his way back to the center. Moreover, Eduardo begins to see himself in this light too:

> On one occasion Perry is trying to remember whose turn it is to place the number tag on the daily calendar. Several students begin to call out, "Eduardo! Eduardo!" indicating that it is Eduardo's turn today. Upon hearing his name called out, though, Eduardo quickly begins to shake his head from side to side and calls out, "No! No!" The plaintive look upon his face seems to indicate that Eduardo feels he is being wrongly accused of something. Eduardo has acceded to the characterization of himself that has been building in the classroom in these early weeks of school.

Perry's reactions and, in turn, those of her other students to Eduardo's behavior have helped to frame his place in school. While Eduardo's case is perhaps extreme in some ways, Eduardo shares with his Canford peers his initial status as an outsider in the group. He often falls outside the boundaries of teachers' expectations in different settings. Eduardo's story highlights how teachers' efforts to bring such students into the fold can in fact push them farther to the outside.

There is no easy solution to working with students like Eduardo. He would likely pose a challenge to most teachers. Teaching is a demanding profession. Balancing the needs of twenty or thirty different students, as well as the curricular demands of the school system, is complicated enough; attending

in particular to a student whose needs are as complicated as
Eduardo's can certainly heighten the challenge. Yet it is important to appreciate what is at stake here and to consider the results for the children involved. If students like Eduardo (in the
Canford Program or elsewhere) are likely to find themselves
struggling from the outset to adapt to the school environment,
what educators consequently do with them has major implications for their experiences at school. The student's success is
contingent on the educator's response. By highlighting Eduardo's status as someone outside the boundaries, his teacher
reinforces his role as an outsider among his peers. It is already
difficult for Canford students and others like them to adapt
and succeed, and teachers who help to label them as outsiders
may well make that task nearly impossible.

VIII
Teaching Styles

The Arbor Town teachers display a range of teaching styles, from a progressive, child-centered, developmental approach to a more traditional, teacher-centered, academically oriented approach. Most teachers employ a variety of methods. Here I describe a typical day in the classrooms of two teachers whose practices generally reflect the two extremes of this continuum, thus setting in relief the features of teaching style that appear to be most relevant to the Canford students' school experiences.

Theresa: Modern Traditionalist

Upon entering Theresa's classroom, one gets a clear sense of order and tidiness. Everything seems to be in its place. Spruce labels have been printed, laminated, and attached to shelves of well-organized materials. Four round tables are arranged neatly in the center of the room, each with its basket of well-ordered student supplies. Students are assigned to table groups and spend much of their time working on tasks at their designated spaces. One corner of the room, occupied by a rectangular rug, is used as a classroom meeting space. Theresa's tidy desk takes up another corner, near the meeting rug. At the other end of the rectangular room are shelves for puzzles and games and an art table near a sink and water fountain.

The following schedule represents a typical morning in Theresa's kindergarten classroom:

> *8:05: Morning Transition.* As students arrive they place their materials in their cubbies and proceed to their assigned tables. Baskets of books selected by Theresa await them. Students sit at their places and read books with their parents. Most of the Canford students look at books by themselves, some with a peer or with their teacher. Although the room is not silent, hardly more than a low hum is discernable.
>
> *8:20: Class Meeting.* Theresa calls the students together to the rug where the class engages in teacher-directed lessons such as calendar activities, songs, and read-alouds. These morning routines can take anywhere from ten to thirty minutes.
>
> *8:40: Directions.* Theresa explains the morning's lesson to her students, which takes another fifteen to twenty minutes. Usually the most substantive academic activities are assigned to this early-morning work period. For example, this morning there are four activities that will all involve patterns:
>
> 1. At one table the students will build patterns with Unifix cubes and then color the same pattern onto a strip of graph paper.

2. Another group will color patterns directly onto a large piece of graph paper.

3. A third group will cut out pictures of different insects from worksheets and paste a pattern of insects onto a large picture of a frog.

4. The last group will build patterns with special blocks of various shapes and colors.

9:00: Table Time Activities. Students are usually in their seats, working on assignments in their table groups. Some time is spent switching tables or activities.

9:50: Cleanup, Snack, and Recess. Theresa goes to the staff lounge during recess. All of the kindergarten students are supervised by teaching assistants during snack and recess time.

10:30: Journal Writing. As students reenter the classroom, they proceed to their tables, where Theresa has placed stacks of writing journals. Students find their own journals and write and illustrate their "news." Theresa and her teaching assistant walk around the classroom and help the students with their writing.

10:50: Class Meeting. Theresa calls the students back to the rug. She shares a storybook with the class, then describes an art and writing activity based on the book.

11:15: Project Time. Students work on their projects at their tables, then clean up.

11:45: Lunch or Early Dismissal.

During the course of the school day in Theresa's classroom, most of the students' time is spent either in teacher-directed activities, such as large group meetings, or in work at assigned table groups. There is little time for student choice or exploration, and the curriculum is focused largely on literacy and mathematics. Spatially, the room is organized in a way that underscores Theresa's priorities. The focus of the room is on the tables where students spend most of their time. Activity spaces such as the art table, the block area, the library, and the playhouse are all confined to the corners, and students spend relatively little time there. In fact, I was in the classroom for nearly two months before I realized that it contained a selection of playhouse toys, as they were hidden in enclosed shelves behind Theresa's desk and were rarely used.

Theresa does offer several breaks from the routine described above. "Free time" is offered once or twice a week, typically as a reward for completing other work or for good behavior. During these periods students may choose from some select activities, such as blocks, games, manipulative toys, and sometimes the playhouse. Other variations occur as well. Once every week or two, the students spend time working in the class garden with parent volunteers, and they have occasional opportunities for art projects and library time. At the end of the year the class works together on a performance of some songs and poetry for the parents.

The following narrative illustrates how one of the Canford students fared in this classroom and teaching environment.

> Amelia is working at her table space, laboring over a patterning and writing activity. Her assignment is to write the letters of her name in a seven-by-seven grid in continuous sequence, beginning with the top left-hand box and proceeding until all forty-nine boxes are filled in. After completing that task, she is expected to use crayons to fill in the boxes using a different color for each letter of her name. In doing

so, the students are expected to notice patterns that emerge in the coloring. Students who complete their projects are allowed to turn their pages over and draw whatever they like.

Amelia has picked up on Theresa's general practice of rewarding early completion of class work with more enticing opportunities, and she has her eyes on the prize. She tells the teaching assistant working with her, " . . . then I do this one, then I do this one, then I get to color on the back!" She flashes a big smile. While Amelia seems to hold out hope that she will finish her spinach in time for dessert, it is clear that the pace of her efforts makes that unlikely. Amelia is a slow writer, and she has a difficult time remaining engaged in this activity, which seems to hold little interest for her aside from the reward of coloring on the back. The teaching assistant works to help keep Amelia on track: "Can you put an 'a' in there?"

Amelia sounds unsure of herself: "An 'a'? There?"

"Yes, put an 'a' there and that's your whole name."

Amelia finishes writing the letter and victoriously calls out, "Done!" She's actually only written her name twice and has quite a way to go before completing the entire assignment—thirty-seven more boxes.

"Great!" replies the teaching assistant. "Now just keep doing that until it's all filled up. Then we can color it in."

Amelia struggles along, but she does not finish the project before Theresa calls out that it is time to clean up and move on to the next activity. "Aw! I didn't get to color," Amelia complains to the teaching assistant.

"You can do it later."

"I want to do it now."

"Well, that's one of the hard parts about kindergarten. You need to follow the directions."

With a disappointed look on her face, Amelia gives the teaching assistant her paper and moves on to the next activity.

Amelia, while fairly adept at following classroom routines compared with many of her Canford peers, often falls behind when it comes to academic work at school. She shares this trait with several of the other Canford students. Amelia persistently pursues the activities set before her, and she clearly wants to succeed, yet she frequently seems to be behind her peers. In addition, as many of the free-choice activities and extended curricula are offered as a bonus for completing primary assignments, Amelia frequently misses out on those opportunities.

Patricia: Old-Fashioned Progressivist

Patricia's classroom is loosely organized around what she calls activity centers. Her oddly shaped classroom space is pocketed with designated centers for art, science, reading, building, games, and dramatic play. A rocking chair sits in front of a set of descending steps where Patricia reads to her students and provides directions for classroom activities. An oval rug sits near the center of the room, where Patricia holds classroom meetings and conducts movement and dance. During most of the day, children are scattered around the classroom at the activity centers and the project tables Patricia has spread out across the room. With an abundant variety of materials in use at any one time, and with students working on disparate activities simultaneously, a sense of loosely ordered chaos reigns in Patricia's classroom.

The following schedule represents a typical morning in Patricia's kindergarten classroom.

> *8:00: Morning Transition.* As students arrive they place their materials in their cubbies and proceed to choose from a number of activities Patricia has provided this morning. Drawing and writing materials are available at two of the project tables, and at another Patricia has set out a plate of crackers and milk for students who may have arrived to school hungry. A few students are in the library reading with their parents. Some others are using magnifying glasses to look at the caterpillars spinning cocoons in the science center. A small group is playing checkers in the Meeting Circle. The room is filled with a subdued early-morning energy as the students warm up for the day.
>
> *8:15: Class Meeting.* Patricia calls the students together to the meeting area. The class begins the day with songs and a story. Patricia also leads her students in several additional morning rituals, such as updating the calendar and reviewing the day's schedule.
>
> *8:30: Movement and Dance.* Patricia extends the group activity into some dancing and movement. Students shuffle, prance, and hop around

the room while Patricia leads them according to the rhythm and story of songs she plays on her compact disc player.

8:45: Directions and Choice Time. After dancing, the students return to the meeting area. Patricia then describes the week's special project. Some students will begin their day by making capes for an autumn festival they will host in their classroom. Other students are assigned to help Patricia's teaching assistant prepare today's snack. The rest are able to select among the various activity center choices, which Patricia reviews with the students. Patricia calls the students one by one. They announce their activity of choice, and Patricia sends them off to "work," as she calls it. A few minutes later, a brief survey of the room reveals the design of Patricia's teaching style. Two students are making prints on their capes with Patricia. The teaching assistant has three students counting out plates and cups and dividing and sorting apples and crackers for snack time. Two other girls are making designs with pattern blocks on one of the project tables. One student is lying on the couch reading a book. Several boys are working together in the block area to make an airport and a control tower. Three students are playing together in the playhouse. Several others are working with the writing and drawing materials at another project table. The classroom is alive with activity.

9:45: Cleanup and Reading. Patricia calls the students back to the meeting area. She assigns cleanup chores to student work groups. After completing their chores, students return to the meeting area and read from books in baskets Patricia has placed on the floor. Once all the students have returned from their cleanup assignments, Patricia dismisses the group to recess.

10:00: Recess and Snack. Patricia and her teaching assistant accompany their students to recess and join them for snack as well.

10:45: Class Meeting. Upon returning to the classroom with her students, Patricia reads a story and then explains today's Table Time activities. During this period students work in small groups on particular assignments that are often, but not always, academic in nature. Today's projects include the following:

1. One group will work on writing and illustrating a page in a classmate's birthday book. In preparation, the students have interviewed the birthday girl earlier in the week and prepared a list of things she enjoys.

2. Another group will be writing and drawing in their journals.

3. The last group will be weaving with yarn, demonstrating various patterns of lines and colors.

11:00: Table Time. Students work on their Table Time activities. Those who complete their assigned project are dismissed to the classroom library.

11:35: Class Meeting. Patricia collects the students back at the meeting area one last time to sing

songs. On early dismissal days, they share good-
byes here to end the day.
11:45: Lunch or Early Dismissal.

Patricia enhances her curriculum with other activities
beyond the daily routine. Once every week or two, Patricia
takes the group on a nature walk in the school's neighborhood.
She usually has a theme or task associated with the walks, such
as collecting leaves to sort in the classroom. The group visits
the school library once a week and regularly engages in art
projects with either Patricia or a specially designated art in-
structor. Patricia organizes several special events during the
course of the year, usually seasonal celebrations involving the
students and their families. Typically the students engage in
special art, writing, and cooking projects as part of the prepa-
rations for these events. Patricia claims that her curriculum is
more "academic" now than it has been in the past, but her
teaching style, classroom organization, and curricular schedule still provide a significant amount of choice for students
within a wide range of opportunities. A longtime teacher near-
ing retirement, Patricia is openly critical of the recent wave of
educational reforms that promote an intense focus on early literacy and a narrowing of the curriculum. She works to retain
much of her own approach to teaching in spite of what she sees
as pressure from district administrators and state officials to
adopt a more rigid and academically oriented program.

The following narrative illustrates how one of the Canford students fared in this learning environment:

During choice time today Patricia has prepared an
art activity as one of the projects available to the
students. The students fold, roll, cut, tear, and paste

together strips of construction paper, fashioning three-dimensional collages of color and shapes. Several students are working at the table constructing their compositions on large black backgrounds of construction paper.

Marcos wanders over to the table. "Can I do this?" he asks Patricia.

"Sure, Marcos. Come and join us," she responds.

Marcos is generally quiet in school. He enjoys a wide range of activities but seems to get frustrated from time to time, particularly with writing projects. He came to kindergarten knowing how to write few letters other than those in his own name, and he often works more slowly and less successfully than his classmates on several of the Table Time projects, such as journals, birthday books, and "letter of the week" activities. At such times, Marcos seems to get dejected. He compares his work unfavorably with that of his peers and sometimes refuses to proceed, claiming, "I can't do this."

As he begins to work on the art project, Marcos takes a long strip of yellow paper and tries to fold it into a staircase as Patricia demonstrated during her initial presentation to the class. Marcos folds the paper in a continuous rather than an alternating pattern, so he ends up with a rolled strip of paper instead of a staircase. He leans over to Patricia and says, "I can't do it! You do it," and he tosses the paper roll down in front of her.

"Sure you can, Marcos," Patricia says. "Let me help you." Patricia takes another strip of paper and hands it to Marcos. She demonstrates the folding pattern for Marcos as she directs him: "Now, make one fold." Marcos follows Patricia's directions. "Now, here comes the tricky part. Turn the strip upside down, then fold again." Marcos continues to follow along, and Patricia nods her head in approval. "Good! Now you're doing it. Just keep turning it over." Marcos finishes the staircase and glues it onto his backdrop. Patricia takes the first strip that Marcos had rolled up and tossed toward her and says, "Oooh! Now look at this, Marcos. You made a spiral!" She loosens up the strip and shows Marcos the spiral design he created. "Maybe you can put that somewhere too."

"Me too!" one of the other students at the table calls out. "I want a spiral too."

"Well, ask Marcos to show you how," Patricia says.

The other student looks at Marcos, who picks up another strip of paper and demonstrates how to make a spiral: "First you do this. Then you do this. Then this," he says as he folds the strip in a continuous loop.

Marcos and the others continue with their projects. At the last class meeting of the day, Patricia has the students share their art projects with the class, and Marcos proudly displays his "Play Castle" to the class, replete with both stairways and spiraling slides.

Marcos has difficulty with some of the assigned activities in his classroom but succeeds in others. He is an avid puzzler, for example, who works on putting together increasingly complicated puzzles over the course of the year. Patricia assists Marcos by providing a diverse set of opportunities in the classroom, thus encouraging him to find his strengths and think of himself as someone who can be successful in the school setting. While he is still behind most of his peers in his writing by the end of the year, he has found other ways to succeed in his classroom.

Opportunities for Learning

Theresa and Patricia's classrooms demonstrate some of the potential impact of teaching styles on the Canford students. Emerging from this portrait are several ways we might think about the construction of educational opportunities for young children.

To begin with, Patricia and Theresa share some features of their teaching styles. Perhaps most notably, children in both classrooms are frequently organized into large-group "class meeting" settings. The teachers use these meetings for telling stories, singing, sharing directions, and performing other classroom rituals and routines. Didactic, teacher-directed lessons like these pervaded all of the classrooms in my study.[1] Another feature common to all of the classrooms was the teachers' prevalent use of complex and lengthy verbal instructions. Teachers would often take upward of fifteen minutes to describe multistep projects and routines. I suspect that many adults would have difficulty accurately recounting such procedures, as many of the students did.

These particular pedagogical features seem to have a great impact on the Canford students. Many of the Canford students have difficulties attending to the long, teacher-directed class meetings. This struggle sets up a pattern of misbehavior followed by the teacher's reprimands or negative labeling. Such a pattern does not bode well for the students' eventual adjustment to the classroom setting. Additionally, classroom environments that rely heavily on teacher-directed discussions and lengthy verbal explanations present problems for English-language learners in particular.

In addition, many of the general rituals and routines in Theresa's and Patricia's classrooms are similar. Both teachers read books aloud to their students quite frequently. They both conduct rituals around a classroom calendar. They both create opportunities for their students to engage in art, science, recreation, and special class projects, though these activities vary in frequency between the two classrooms.

In spite of these commonalities, there is quite a contrast between the types of opportunities afforded to the students in the two classrooms. The ranges of curricular opportunities are quite different, and other less obvious differences exist as well. For example, students in Patricia's classroom have more opportunities to interact with a wide range of curricular materials and are offered more ways to express and explore their interests and to find their personal strengths and preferences. Patricia's students also have significantly greater opportunities for making their own choices, experiencing variation in educational settings, and communicating and collaborating with their peers.

When students like Amelia spend much of their time in school pursuing activities in which they experience early and frequent failure, what do they learn about themselves, about school, and about the priorities of the community and larger society? A more robust set of learning opportunities might support a wider range of student strengths, interests, and needs, and foster a sense of success and belonging among a larger number of school children.

The primary point here is that the teacher's approach to the arrangement of learning opportunities clearly has an impact on the experiences of students. Based on my observations, I would argue that students who tend to be outsiders from the outset need a wide range of occasions for interacting, sharing, struggling, and exploring, all with the conscious guidance and support of a strong teacher. Such opportunities help students develop a greater ability to learn and practice the skills necessary for fitting in and excelling in the school setting. If students are confined to a narrow type of activity settings, it is likely that more of them are liable to find failure and frustration, particularly those students who arrive without familiarity with the practices essential to success in that kind of work.

An Apprenticeship of Schooling

An apprenticeship framework may provide a useful model for understanding the struggles of the Canford students. An apprenticeship is generally a process through which a novice becomes more expert in a particular practice through active participation and with the guidance and support of an expert in the field. In writing about apprenticeship situations and the development of membership in communities of practice, Lave and Wenger (1991) articulate a notion of "legitimate peripheral participation." Broadly summarized, this concept describes how nascent members of a community move from practicing and learning on the periphery of an enterprise toward holding more central roles in a community of shared values, understandings, and practices.[2]

In this conception, apprentices may work *legitimately* on

the edges of a community, learning its core set of skills, practices, and shared understandings as they grow into more central roles. Work on the periphery is valued by the community as an essential component of developing expertise and full participating membership. Over time, apprentices are supported to move toward more central participation. In the words of Lave and Wenger: "The key to legitimate peripherality is access by newcomers to the community of practice and all that membership entails. . . . To become a full member of a community of practice requires access to a wide range of ongoing activity, old-timers, and other members of the community; and to information, resources, and opportunities for participation" (100 – 101).

I believe that this concept also provides a useful framework for thinking about the Canford students and others who struggle in the school setting to move from peripheral participation to more central roles. In Lave and Wenger's formulation, one's status as a novice is viewed as a natural place on the path toward expertise. One is not expected to enter a community of practice fully prepared to take on the roles and responsibilities of an expert. Novices are understood to require access to information, resources, opportunities for participation, and the support and guidance of experts. Without these elements, full membership in a community of practice is unlikely.

It is not all that clear that they could be called legitimate peripheral participants in the school setting. Their status might be better described as a static form of peripherality, as they tend to remain on the outside with limited access to many of the essential tools for successful adaptation. Moreover, the view of many of the "experts" in this setting is that the students' outsider status is a permanent condition rather than a precursor to competence. From the apprenticeship perspective, though, the static nature of peripherality is not a deficient quality of the students in any way, but rather an indicator of insufficient apprenticeship as organized by the adults in the educational system.

Considered from the apprenticeship point of view, teachers and other adults play, or should play, a key role as veterans and experts, monitoring access to important tools, information, and cultural knowledge. The more they actively and intentionally provide for and support the apprenticeships of their students, the better that these children will be able to take on central roles in multiple venues.

One could argue, then, that a significant constraint on the successful adjustment to the school setting for the Canford students is the existence of an unacknowledged and insufficient apprenticeship. An affirming and supportive apprenticeship association—one that would help make the subtle and implicit rules and expectations of school more clear and explicit—could provide for a more successful school transition for these students.

Admittedly, the analogy between students and apprentices is imperfect. Schools are not designed for (novice) students to become (master) teachers. At the same time, they *are* designed for students to acquire many of the skills, practices, and understandings of their teachers, not only academic knowledge but also civic, social, and moral skills and dispositions. Thus in a broad sense the apprenticeship model helps to illuminate the experience of students.

Several examples from earlier chapters highlight the ways a better-supported apprenticeship may help the Canford students more successfully navigate the obstacle course of schooling. For example, the librarian working with Marikit and Tali (see chapter 5) may have better appreciated the peripheral nature of their participation in the story-time setting and either expanded her conception of appropriate practices or better helped facilitate those students' grasp of expected routines and practices. Further, in several places I describe settings in which students are regularly left to sort out events, routines, and relationships among themselves, such as the bus rides, snack time, and the playground (see chapters 3 and 4). Understanding the work of these youngsters as analogous to an apprenticeship would suggest a greater role in such venues by experts who can help them sort out effective strategies and practices for long-term success.

An additional puzzle here is that the expectations of teachers and of the school system do not always mirror our society's best hopes for children and schools. Still, a clearer acknowledgment of an apprenticeship model is likely to encourage educators to look more carefully at their routines and practices and be more deliberate about them than they might otherwise be.

Other scholars use the framework of social or cultural capital to help explain the difficulties children like the Canford students encounter.[3] I believe that these concepts provide a valuable contribution to understanding the Canford students and others but assign too much importance to the character traits and social connections of the children themselves. This view of the problem in turn suggests solutions that place too great a burden on students, their families, and their communities to transform. In contrast, an apprenticeship view places the locus of responsibility on the educators. One should rightfully expect that students might arrive at the school setting ill-prepared to master the domains and tasks before them. What they need to succeed is access to proper tools, resources, information, and guidance. Educators—the experts in this apprenticeship model—are responsible for helping to provide this access.

As a final note, an apprenticeship model is also useful in that it encompasses a more complete understanding of the multifaceted undertaking that school represents for students. Children learn about their place in school and relationships with peers while also acquiring skills and practices deemed valuable and important by the larger society. We want students to thrive in a multiplicity of ways—academically, socially, emotionally, democratically, and otherwise. Schooling is about more than just learning to read and write. An apprenticeship view of schooling can include these broader social and cultural aims of the educational endeavor, as well as any particular skill set one might wish to impart.

IX
The Road Ahead

At least on the surface, the Canford Program resonates with promise and opportunity. A group of motivated parents makes an active choice to take advantage of what appears to be a better educational opportunity for their children by transferring them out of an impoverished and poor-performing school district and into a neighboring district that is well resourced and high achieving. These parents have high hopes and a high regard for the American ideal of greater opportunity and prosperity through educational attainment. I do not believe that the experiences of the Canford students diminish those aspirations, but I do hope that my observations provide a fuller appreciation of the road these children travel in striving for those objectives.

More to the point, what does an examination of the richness and complexity of these children's experiences have to teach us about the circumstances of this particular program and about the wider American educational enterprise? In this final chapter I discuss some of the conclusions and implications I draw from this work.

Expanding Our View of Schooling

The Canford students' school day commences at the bus stop and includes a wide array of experiences both within and beyond the walls of their classrooms. If nothing else, the exploits of the Canford students demonstrate for us the rich and complex nature of schooling. While the proposition that the endeavor of schooling is a multifaceted one may sound straightforward, much of our educational policy, practice, and research, not to mention our standards of achievement and tools for assessment, seems to belie this point.

One of the principal aims of our public school system is the development of an engaged and productive citizenry, one that can support and strengthen our pluralistic, democratic society. Although basic literacy is obviously an indispensable outcome of a successful education, schooling does not begin and end with learning to read and calculate. A large part of the undertaking of the students in this study is learning how to adapt to and succeed in a novel environment. They are working to navigate the complex obstacle course of schooling, which entails much more than the successful acquisition of a set of academic skills and abilities. Social, emotional, procedural, and cultural practices, among others, are equally relevant to the students in this setting, if not more so. Fostering additional aptitudes and inclinations, such as creativity, civility, and democratic values, are also worthy aims of public schools. To the degree that schools and educational systems are focused on a narrow range of academic goals, they either ignore or undermine these broader endeavors that are essential to the future success of students and of our pluralistic, democratic society. If we, as educators, want our students to flourish and our democracy to thrive, we would do well to acknowledge and embrace a wider view of the educational experience.

We should also consider more carefully the Herculean task that these young students are asked to tackle. Are the subtle and implicit rules and expectations that we employ warranted? Are they useful? Are they beneficial to our educational aims? Are they realistic? What can we do to help students master them? When we put young children in the position of sorting out the difference between appropriately "laughing at the story" and "interrupting the whole story" we need to think carefully about what we are truly asking them to learn and what our own role is in helping them to master that lesson. A conception of teaching in an apprenticeship framework could be useful in this regard, as it places a more direct responsibility on educators to sort out what practices, skills, and understandings their students need and then to determine how best to help the students acquire them. Successful navigation of the obstacle course requires more explicit guideposts, published rulebooks, effective coaches and mentors, appropriate nutrition, and cheering crowds along the way. If our society mandates that young children engage in this contest, it is our duty to furnish the prerequisites for a successful outcome.

One of my objectives in the design and form of this research endeavor was to account for the broad set of experiences relevant to the students in the Canford Program. Factors such as social engagement, emotional connections, cultural bridges and barriers, teaching styles, individual student strengths and needs, and opportunities for learning are all pertinent in elucidating the educational experience of youngsters, as well as in considering how to measure the outcomes of educational programs. To account for the impact of an hour-long bus ride or the complexities of building friendships across cultural, linguistic, geographic, and socioeconomic barriers, one must rely on a more holistic set of tools and lenses than the narrow, standardized measures of academic achievement. While academic measures are certainly valuable to the field, studies focused on the day-to-day experiences of students are far too rare, especially in the earliest grades. We need to conceive of approaches to policy, assessment, and research that better account for the elaborate nature of the educational enterprise. It is my hope and belief that by striving to broaden our scope of inquiry we will serve the diverse needs of our children and the educational aims of our society in a more thoughtful and comprehensive manner.

Embracing the Challenge of Diversity

Over the past century, our schools have been tasked with educating a rising proportion of our nation's youth, one that is increasingly diverse and possesses a wide range of strengths, interests, and needs. This challenge is daunting, and we have yet to meet it sufficiently. Yet we are most likely to do so if we genuinely acknowledge and embrace the tasks before us. As educators, we must grapple with the responsibility to engage a diverse student population and prepare them all for successful roles in our society.

Undoubtedly the experiences of the Canford students suggest that teachers and administrators should more carefully consider the difficulties involved in the social integration of students from different community, cultural, or linguistic backgrounds. Programs of school desegregation, whether voluntary or mandatory, are designed as social engineering projects. Typically, schools pay most heed to moving students from one place to another (desegregation), neglecting the social and interactional aspects of schooling (integration) that may be at least equally important to the success of the students. These aspects are likely given inadequate attention because they are more complicated and perhaps more controversial than the basic process of transferring students. Yet, if social and political progress is a worthy goal of the system, which I believe it is, then we would do well to attend more closely to these arenas. For instance, other transfer and desegregation programs orchestrate mentor-type relationships among students or families from different communities.[1] Such arrangements help foster better social connections between transfer students and their new schools and communities. Other elements of integration, such as better inclusion of children and their families in social and after-school opportunities, may be complicated, but they are clearly supportive of students' adaptation to and success in the setting.

Moreover, teachers and school administrators must be willing to openly address and confront issues of race and class and other forms of diversity. This stance is particularly important to a program specifically designed in response to problems of racial segregation and educational inequity. The opening of a door of opportunity is, in and of itself, insufficient to the task.

Further, a heterogeneous student population demands a multifaceted approach to teaching. Understanding that what works for some students may not work for everyone is critical.[2] Knowledge of the diverse strengths, interests, and needs of students, as well as familiarity with their families and communities, must inform the teacher's instructional strategy. While all students require a healthy diet, not everyone will thrive on any one particular recipe.

Finally, we must appreciate that on some level *all* schools face this challenge. Every educator is tasked with supporting the diverse needs of students in some way or another. None of us are exempt from these demands.

Recognizing Areas of Educational Neglect

The students in this study spent a significant portion of their school day in what I would consider educationally neglected activities such as the bus ride, recess, lunch and snack breaks, free choice and free play times in classrooms, and multiple transitional events. If we tallied up the allotted school hours students spent in these various activities, we would likely be quite surprised at the results. For example, in a cursory review of Paloma's twelve-hour school day (see chapter 5), I estimated that she spent roughly half her time in activities and spaces to which scant attention is being paid from an educational standpoint. All of these activities could be purposefully supervised and guided, but more frequently they are only loosely supervised or completely neglected. More significant, they are rarely arranged with any larger educational goals in mind.

Bus trips, for example, are incredibly expensive in terms of not only capital expenditures but also the enormous opportunity costs they impose on children. Some of the students in this study spent up to two hours on the bus and at bus stops over the course of their school day. These spaces are wholly neglected from an educational standpoint, yet as Dewey (1938) suggested, these children are engaged in important experiences, and from those experiences they are learning *something*. The issue is the character and quality of those experiences and their "educative" or "mis-educative" disposition.

A five-year-old student who gets on the bus at 6:55 A.M. for an hour-long bus ride does not distinguish between the transportation process and the more traditional schooling experiences to be found at the schoolhouse on the other end of the ride. When the large yellow bus with the word SCHOOL printed in bold black letters on its side drives up to the stop, the school day has plainly begun for this child. If he or she steps off the bus an hour later tired, hungry, and scared and brings these dispositions into the classroom, educators must be prepared to attend to and account for these effects.

The impact of such educationally neglected spaces is discernable and significant, and consequently they demand more of our attention. What do the students who ride the bus for two hours a day, with a threat of harassment and a general sense of discomfort, learn about what it means to adapt and succeed? What do they learn about the school system that orchestrates this experience for them? What might they be learning about themselves? Education or miseducation occurs in a wide array of activity settings, too many of which we orchestrate on children's behalf but with little thought or attention.

Some implications of these circumstances are quite direct. For example, the Canford students' experiences varied considerably in the transition onto and off the bus at the school sites. Having a teacher, another adult, or even an older student at the bus stop to greet and attend to new and young students would be an uncomplicated potential enhancement for participating children. Other considerations are more complex but are still warranted. For example, policy makers considering school choice programs as a mechanism for enhancing educational opportunities for children must think seriously about the means, as well as the ends, involved in their decisions. Complex tradeoffs abound and need to be considered more thoughtfully. For example, do we really want to impose on our youth the kinds of conditions I described on the bus? What are the costs to them and to us in the long run? Are supervisors on the bus warranted, as some school districts have determined? Are shorter routes needed? What about providing actual educational opportunities during the bus ride? Offering educational videos or a daily news show along with some minimal supervision to monitor student safety and security would be a useful starting point. Other practical enhancements could surely be construed with some attention and creativity focused on the problem.

Similarly, playgrounds are highly consequential school settings that are often largely ignored from an educational standpoint. Small numbers of untrained assistants are commonly provided to supervise the activities of large numbers of children during snack, lunch, and recess breaks in our schools. Are such arrangements sufficient to meet students' needs? Are they appropriate or even safe? Who, then, teaches the youngest participants in such settings the appropriate rules of engagement? Do we want to place such responsibility on the shoulders of other children? If so, do we want to do so without appropriately preparing them for the task? Some schools have tended to such dilemmas by implementing conflict resolution programs, training peer mediators to assist in playground supervision, and organizing intramurals and other structured clubs and activities. More focused and sustained consideration, though, is still needed in this regard. We cannot afford to exclude from our educational considerations these tangential yet meaningful experiences and their impact on our children.

These educationally neglected spaces are especially significant for the very youngest students in our schools and for others likely to find themselves on the outside of implicit understandings and behaviors. If we think again about the apprenticeship relationships these students have within schools, who are their "masters" in these settings? Who imparts the wisdom, practices, and ways of being to help them learn to thrive and succeed? Do we really want to consign our children to such an unstructured set of activities? I am not suggesting that we program and routinize every moment of the school day for children. Mistakes, risks, uncertainty, choice, and opportunity are all formative elements of learning, growth, and human development. Yet we should be more thoughtful about how, when, and why we provide for different kinds of experiences and opportunities in schools.

Appreciating the Importance of Teaching

Of all the aspects of the educational system, the quality of teaching has the greatest impact on the achievement of students.[3] Teachers in my study influenced the experience of the Canford students in several important ways, either encouraging their engagement with and adaptation to their school or further marginalizing them. Teachers' attitudes and perspectives, roles as perceptual leaders, and orchestration of learning opportunities in and out of the classroom all had important implications for the quality of the Canford students' school experiences.

These elements in the relationship between teachers and their students have enormous relevance for the organization of the teaching profession, from preparation through retirement. As a consequence, we must thoughtfully orchestrate the conditions and opportunities for teacher education, professional development, professionalization, and advancement in ways that work to sustain the purposes of our educational system.

Further, we need to uncover, examine, and reconsider long-held assumptions about and proclivities in teaching that may not support the needs of our students. Examples might include the organization of students into narrow age-graded cohorts or passive, teacher-directed pedagogy. In addition, can we rightfully expect one classroom teacher charged with the

care of twenty to thirty diverse pupils to meet all of their disparate needs as well as the curricular demands of state and federal policy makers? Might our students be better served, for
example, by teams of teachers who share responsibility for student development yet each possess a narrower but deeper
knowledge base? In so doing we may find new and more fruit-
ful approaches. We are more likely to engage and foster success
in a wider range of students through a conception of teaching
and schooling that respects and encourages the imaginative
and the exploratory; one that is less concerned with codes, rules,
and competition; and one that engages the social, physical,
aesthetic, affective, and moral realms of human development
as well as the intellectual. The current tenor of the educational
times, with a hyperattentiveness to a narrow range of academic pursuits and a focus on high-stakes testing, even of our
very youngest students, pushes in the opposite direction, to the
detriment of our children and our larger society.

A Word about School Choice

The current political and educational landscape portends an
increase in educational "choice" programs, be they voucher
programs, charter schools, voluntary transfer opportunities
like Canford, or others. To date, we have mustered insufficient
research and understanding about the experiences or outcomes such programs engender. Given this fact, we must do
more to take stock of what the experience is like for students
who participate in these social, political, and educational ex-
periments, as well as look at their academic achievement, high
school and college graduation rates, and other indices of short-
and long-term outcomes.[4]

My work with the Canford families offers a few relevant
insights. First, it seems clear that given what is considered an

unambiguously and significantly superior educational opportunity for their children, parents are willing to take advantage of this type of educational choice program. At the same time, we should note that the decision-making process of these parents relied primarily on two factors: word of mouth and standardized test scores. For the most part, parents considered no other potentially relevant factors in making their decisions. Were the choice more subtle or the decision more complicated, how would parents act? Many proponents of educational choice programs place a great deal of weight on the efficiencies of a market-driven system. At their best, though, markets rely on informed actors making rational choices based on easily accessible information. The decisions of the parents in this study suggest both that their choices are based on a limited set of information and that acquiring further information to support decision making is quite difficult, if not impossible.

In addition, parents and educators engaged in educational opportunities that require students to navigate across community boundaries need to better understand and prepare for the potential complications involved. The successful transfer from South Bay City schools to those in Arbor Town requires more than an opening of doors and an affordance of opportunity. If parents and teachers were better informed about the potential tradeoffs and difficulties such choices encompass, they might be better prepared to ameliorate some of the problems engendered by community separation, boundary crossing, lengthy bus rides, and other complications. Further, some basic functions and responsibilities of schools are noticeably more difficult when transfer students are involved. For instance, in the Canford Program, communication between home and school frequently faltered because of geographic isolation or linguistic and cultural barriers. Devoting additional time and resources to projects such as the translation of notes and newsletters, the development of better communication systems, and the creation of more frequent opportunities for families to participate in their children's school is clearly warranted, and these steps seem more likely to be established if a wider range of issues are accounted for at the inception of such programs.

Conclusion

Broadly summarized, the primary conclusion of this study is that this program developed to facilitate the integration of diverse students across district boundaries tends to have the somewhat ironic effect of creating additional stress, hardships, complications, and even marginalization for participating students. The issues raised here have implications for the structure and goals of schooling, the means and measures of success, the tools and uses of assessment, the preparation and support of teachers, and more. Developing solutions to such puzzles will be demanding. It will require a great deal more study and not a small amount of ingenuity. Further, when such efforts are implemented, they invariably will entail choices and tradeoffs, and the end results will remain messy. Still, we cannot afford to continue to rely on unwarranted traditions, habits, and assumptions. I think it is clear that attending to such matters is crucial to the educational opportunities and aspirations of our nation's youth. My hope is that we will do so while keeping the experiences and struggles of the Canford students in mind, and that we will work to develop and support teachers, schools, and approaches to education that are increasingly designed for the success of all of our children.

Appendix

Notes on Method

Miles Davis often commented to band members, "You need to know your horn, know the chords, know all the tunes. Then you forget about all that, and just play." The same is true of doing fieldwork. Generating data requires constant improvisation, but improvisation requires all the skills.
—Graue and Walsh (1998), 102

In *The Nature of Interpretation in Qualitative Research* (2000), Alan Peshkin reflects on the interaction between the researcher's subjective self and his field of study, noting how every action, choice, and interpretation affects the quality and product of our endeavors. As Peshkin states, "An important reason for reflecting on the development of an interpretation is to show the way a researcher's self, or identity in a situation, intertwines with his or her understanding of the object of the investigation" (5). Throughout the process of completing this study and writing this book, I have attempted to maintain a reflective stance toward these efforts in order to better understand, appreciate, and account for the interaction between my own subjective self as a researcher and the product of my efforts. Though perhaps it goes without saying, the stories I share here are *an* account of the Canford students, not *the* account. In making judgments, interpretations, and decisions, both of selection and of omission, I have fundamentally shaped the work presented here. I believe this fact to be true of all research endeavors: they are the product of both the subject and the researcher. Toward that end, I think it appropriate to share with the reader some of the key decisions made in the methodology and manufacture of this work.

Methods

*Every method of data collection is only an approximation to
knowledge. Each provides a different and usually valid glimpse
of reality, and all are limited when used alone.*
—Warwick (1973), p. 190

With the help of district and school level administrators and the agreement
of classroom teachers and participating parents, I closely observed and interacted with eleven kindergarten students in the Canford Program over the
course of one full academic year. I conducted this work in five classrooms at
two different school sites in the Arbor Town school district. I spent between
one and five days a week at the school sites, and I have estimated that my observations covered approximately three hundred hours in the field. In effect,
the research project lasted two years, as I also conducted a year-long pilot
study with two additional students in one of the same classrooms.

I relied on participant observation in the school setting as my primary
research tool, although observations also extended outside of school to bus
rides, after-school programs, and students' homes for interviews with parents.

My roles in the capacity of a participant observer varied tremen-
dously. I infrequently became the proverbial "fly on the wall," observing and
recording notes from the periphery. At other times I played a more direct
role in leading small group activities with students or providing direct super-
visory support at the behest of classroom teachers. Most often, I found myself
situated somewhere between these two extremes. I had an active but ill-defined
set of roles in the classroom. My roles were structured by my research questions and interests, by the teachers who were my hosts, and by the needs and
demands of the students. As Graue and Walsh (1998) aptly state, "Because interpretive research comes out of interactions among people, role construction is an ongoing process. Needs of participants shift over time as conditions
change, physical demands shift, and relationships build, rupture, and are re-
paired. Role negotiation occurs repeatedly over the course of a study" (76).

The definition and fulfillment of roles were a constant and ongoing
source of negotiation in my fieldwork. Here are just a few examples of the
multiple roles I was asked to play in the conduct of my research: supporter
("Can you tie my shoes?"), expert ("How do you spell 'read'?"), boundary interpreter ("Can I go play in Mary's classroom?"), playmate ("Do you want to
play 'house'?"), confidant ("Know what my brother does sometimes?"), conflict
resolver ("Stacy took my shovel!"), helper ("Will you read me a book?"), friend
("Can I sit with you?"), supervisor ("Would you mind walking with Talya up to
the office?"), and teacher ("Can you lead this activity group today?").

There were both benefits and drawbacks to playing these multiple roles. Doing so provided me with access, proximity, and a sense of belonging, all of which were essential for my ability to conduct my fieldwork. At the same time, some of the roles I played potentially conflicted with my research goals. When students saw me as a teacher or a disciplinarian was I less likely to see full or authentic interactions than when they saw me as a friend or a researcher? Which roles should I shy away from? Which ones should I embrace? These are questions I constantly struggled with in my work.

Beyond my role as a participant observer, I employed a host of other research tools to enhance my understanding of the experiences of these students and to sharpen and triangulate my analyses. These other methods included intensive "shadowing" of individual students; semistructured interviews with students, parents, teachers, and administrators; artifact-based and storytelling interviews with students; the general collection of such artifacts as classroom newsletters, parent notices, and program descriptions; and some basic historical research. Each of these approaches provided a unique window into the educational endeavors of the Canford students.[1]

In fashioning a coherent whole from the collage of information I gathered during my fieldwork, I relied on an ongoing cycle of data collection, analysis, interpretation, critical skepticism, and reflection. As Taylor and Bogdan (1998) describe it, "Qualitative data analysis . . . is not fundamentally a mechanical or technical process; it is a process of inductive reasoning, thinking, and theorizing."

In *The Enlightened Eye* (1998) Eisner offers three sources of evidence that qualitative researchers can rely on to meet "reasonable standards of credibility," and my hope is that this work satisfies these criteria. "Structural corroboration" suggests the use of multiple sources of data in making claims about a topic or subject. "Consensual validation" calls for the agreement among qualified others that the work is meritorious. Thus, the support of both academic and practitioner colleagues in this effort has been invaluable. Finally, works that are able to enhance the perception of a particular phenomenon are said to possess "referential adequacy." If in the end I have crafted an account, supported by evidence from my fieldwork, that illuminates the experience of the Canford students in a way that is cogent, credible, and captivating, I will consider this book a success.

The Participants

I was guided by several factors in selecting participants for this study. Primarily, I wanted to work with students who would be reasonably representative of the general population of Canford students. Ethnically, the program's participants are quite diverse, as is the group of students in my study

Table A.1   Study Participant Demographic Information

	Study Participants	Canford Overall	Arbor Town Elementary
Male:Female	~ 3:2	~ 1:1	~ 1:1
Caucasian	0%	0%	64%
African American	23%	24%	4%
Hispanic	62%	57%	9%
Other	15%	19%	23%
English Language Learner	69%	over 50%	n/a

Source: Data from County Compliance Report (2001–2002) and personal communication with Arbor Town district officials (2003).

(table A.1). Further, most Canford students use school district busing as a means of transportation, rely on the subsidized school lunch program, and are likely to know few, if any, other entering kindergarten students at the beginning of the school year. The students in my study are again representative of the larger group in these ways. Student participation in the study was contingent on parental consent. I worked with district administrators and school principals identifying schools, classrooms, and teachers with whom I might work. Teachers offered their own informed consent as well.

Quandaries

> *Doing research with young children is as complex, rewarding, and messy as living and working with them. It takes a keen eye to their needs, rather than to needs of the research project. It requires attention to the special circumstances that allow children to show us their worlds.*
> —Graue and Walsh (1998), 13

There are inevitable ethical and practical tensions in all research, but perhaps more so in qualitative research studies. Moreover, because of the age of my primary participants, issues such as confidentiality, informed consent, and the impact of the research on the participants were more sensitive. As Eisner (1998) suggests, researchers may never be able to reach an ethical ideal, but we do work under an imperative to be vigilant in our consciousness of such concerns.

In three areas in particular, my principal research methods and the young age of my primary participants combined to create certain ethical and procedural dilemmas. These areas include the development of relationships with the participants in my study, the definition and assignment of roles for myself in the field, and the potential influence that I may have exerted on the experience of my participants in conducting this research.

To begin with, in order to gain the necessary level of access to students and their environments, I developed relationships with them. As in all relationships, particularly ones with young children, we needed to build trust, clarify boundaries, and so on. For my part these relationships also entailed the playing of multiple roles, as I described earlier, many of which do not fit neatly into an idealized paradigm of researcher-subject relationships. In filling these multiple roles, I came at times to question the impact I might be having on the students in my study.

As the following quotes from two of the kindergarten teachers indicate, my place in the classroom was not uninvolved. I was an active participant observer in the pursuit of this project, and as such my presence was noted by the study's participants in various ways. Several of the teachers commented positively about my presence and impact in their classrooms. Allison, for example, said, "Oh, they love to be, well, everybody wants to be with you. The Canford kids, I think they see you as a really good friend, an ally in this strange world. So they saw you, and their eyes would light up."

And Pam claimed, "I think for all the kids, they just liked when you came. They would say, 'Oh, Ira!' You know? Even today when Carrie saw you, she's like, 'Oh, it's Ira!' I think it was just a positive thing for them all, just to have another adult helper around."

On the other hand, some teachers also noted that my presence could be disruptive at times. As Georgia said, "Oh, they got used to you. The more you're around the better it is, so they don't get too excited."

Moreover, while most of the teachers claimed that because of the extended nature of my participant observation I became a "natural" and unobtrusive part of the environment, at least one teacher felt that my presence heightened her consideration of the Canford students in her classroom: "I think when you're here, I tend to look at the Canford kids more. I know you're here to mainly look at them, so I look at them too, to make sure that they're on, like doing what they should be doing, but, yeah, it calls attention to them more for me. I think I focus more on them than the other students, like, not totally on them, but I do make it a point, because I know you're here watching them, and I want to see what they're doing and what you see that they're doing. So . . . it's not like I don't watch them, you know, regardless, but I spent extra time, I think, when you're here watching them."

Impact of the Researcher

Researcher as Friend and Supporter

In some ways I became one of the more reliable "friends" for the Canford students. My relationships with these children, while perhaps less fulfilling for them than connections they might make to their own peers, had the advantages of stability and consistency. For some students, one of their earliest strong personal connections in the school setting was with me. For example, over the first several months of school, when I came into his classroom, Felix would often run to my side, calling "Ira! Ira!" and would pull me over to join in his activity. On several occasions when I went to interact with other students, he would call out, "Play with *me*, Ira! Play with *me!*" hoping perhaps to protect his special connection to me from the intrusion of others.

This kind of "special friend" relationship was evidenced in many ways. I often walked the Canford students to and from the bus stop or back and forth from their lesson with a language or academic tutor. I frequently stood next to them in line during transitions or helped them with chores and classroom activities. I interacted with the students in supportive roles by assisting them with academic work, connecting socially during snack and play times, and helping with mundane tasks such as tying shoes and carrying backpacks. By being a special friend to Felix and others I surely provided something unique in their experiences at school. Can I measure or account for that contribution specifically? I am doubtful. What I can do is give some accounting here that helps to round out the picture of the experiences of these students including some of the ways that I may have affected those experiences myself. I have broadly divided my inquiry here into two categories: ways in which I may have eased or enhanced the experience for these students, and ways in which I may have made things more difficult.

Researcher as Catalyst

Clearly I made some things easier or more comfortable for the students from time to time. I often wondered if in some ways I may have played a role in the social lives of the Canford students more significant than that of an assistant or a special friend. For many different reasons, as some of the teachers indicated, I was often an appealing playmate for many students in the classrooms in which I worked. That fact, coupled with the fact that I spent a good deal of time in the vicinity of the Canford students, may well have brought students together who would not have found one another otherwise. Here is one such example from my field notes:

> Felix is playing by himself in the block area during free choice time. I sit down near him and begin making another tower beside his. In this way, I gain access to Felix and can engage him in conversation. Soon, Bobby and Taylor come to the block area. Taylor in particular likes to build with me as well. "What are you doing?" Taylor asks. It is unclear if he is asking Felix or me or both. I look at Felix, who says, "We're doing blocks," without looking up from his work. Taylor looks at me and asks, "Can we build too?" "Sure," I say, and I move over to create a space for Bobby and Taylor that might also involve Felix in the play. Later, Felix suggests that he and I connect our two towers with a road. Taylor asks if he and Bobby can connect their buildings to mine as well. As we work, Bobby suggests that we make an additional road connecting their building to Felix's. The boys become very excited about the project, and later as I slip away they continue to work together in the block area.

So, at least in part, I played the dual roles of common friend and of facilitator in the social arrangements of these students. Facilitating was not my primary role or responsibility in the conduct of my research, but it was perhaps a significant one in some ways. One of the teachers noted a similar effect: "You know, sometimes just having you sitting down and playing with them makes somebody else come over. 'Oh, what are they doing?' And that is really good. And it gives them kind of a special buddy and a guy, you know, not another woman, for them to pal around with, you know, they really like that. Wouldn't it be wonderful if we had somebody in each school, like you, that that was their job?"

While I did not see my "job" as working directly to foster relationships between Canford students and their school peers, there were times when my presence seemed to support that cause.

Researcher as Impediment

At the same time, I sometimes questioned whether my relationships with the Canford students impeded their interactions with and connections to their peers. Hector, for example, was one of the Canford students who had a difficult time connecting with others. On the days that I was present during recess, he nearly always sought out my companionship.

I walk outside the door to the sand playground, where I find
Anita's class actively engaged in recess. Hector is pacing the
blacktop, kicking up sand with his shoes, his head down. When
he looks up, we see one another, and a wide grin spreads across
his face. Hector quickly walks toward me. "You want to play
with me?" he asks. I agree, and we build castles together in the
sandbox for a while. Later that same morning, Hector finds me
again. "Do you want to wash the flowers with me?" he asks, and
we work together on another activity. At the end of the play period, Hector finds me one last time. "Do you want to play hide
and seeks?" he requests. Again I agree to join him, this time
suggesting that we invite some other nearby children to play
with us as well.

Hector seems to be looking for a friend, and I oblige, but am I helping or hurting him by playing this role? Hector and the other Canford students often had a difficult time connecting to the social center of play at
school. Do I provide a useful opportunity for him to find social success in
this venue, or do I diminish his opportunities for interacting with his peers
by allowing him to take up his time with me? These questions pestered me
throughout my research, and I am still uncertain of the answers. Yet they are
important to consider and pursue. I think it is important that, in talking
about influential adults in the schooling of the Canford students in my
study, I account for myself as well as the others in this endeavor.

Looking in the Mirror

*We also list three basic assumptions underlying fieldwork—the kids are
smart, they make sense, and they want to have a good life. A humble researcher who
respects the kids who host her as smart, sensible, and
desirous of a good life will be ethical in her relationship with them.*
—McDermott, as cited in Graue and Walsh (1998), 57.

What should one make of all of these quandaries and complications? In the
end, what is the sum impact of these issues on the story of the Canford students I relate here? Unfortunately, these questions are not easily or neatly an-
swered. Clearly, I too played a role in the lives of the Canford students during the course of this study. Moreover, as a researcher, I brought a set of
perspectives, attitudes, teaching styles, and the like—my "subjectivities"—to
the task.[2] While the focus of this effort remains the experiences of the Canford students themselves, I think it is worth noting some of the potential is-

sues and dilemmas and the possible impact of my own role in this story, and toward that end I have attempted to explicate some of the ways my presence in the field may have exerted some influence on the subject I sought to explore. At the same time I believe that, on balance, my role in this story is one of a minor, even marginal, character. The larger forces at play that I have noted and described throughout this work were predominant in the lives of these students.

The main point here is that researchers can and do have an impact on the course of their work, whether it be through the conduct of the inquiry itself, the creation of the forms of representation of the work, or the subtle choices of inclusion, exclusion, voice, emphasis, and the like. It would be naïve, perhaps even disingenuous, to claim otherwise. Consequently, I believe it is in order to briefly account for, or at least take an account of, some of the ways in which I, as a researcher, may have played a role in the story I pursued and share here. I am not sure that one can measure and justify all such effects of the researcher's involvement, but acknowledging and tending to the subject is a useful and important start.

Writing

Writing is a craft, and it entails choices of content, form, structure, emphasis, voice, and style, among others. As Eisner (1997) notes, "The selection of a form of representation, whether by mindless habit or by reflective choice, affects what we see" (7). Consequently, it is worth sharing some elements of the choices involved in developing this particular text. First, as noted earlier, to one degree or another I have altered the names and distinguishing characteristics of the students, parents, teachers, and administrators with whom I worked in order to protect their anonymity. I felt a special obligation in regard to confidentiality, since the primary participants in this study were too young to offer their own fully informed consent.[3] Sources in the reference list referring to districts, localities, and programs also reflect these pseudonyms. All quotations and descriptions of events are an accurate reflection of my best attempts at thorough and precise documentation.

Making choices in terminology often proved a daunting and difficult task, one fraught with the peril of unintended meanings and consequences. In their work, McDermott (1987) and Varenne and McDermott (1998) make the broader argument that the social and political forces that help to shape the structures and procedures of schooling also tend to have significant negative consequences for particular students, specifically through the mechanism of labeling (the use of the term "disability," for example), which then limits those students' opportunities for success. In thinking about my work along these lines, I have tried to be as thoughtful and accurate as possible. Fortunately and unfortunately, many words have multiple meanings and may well convey messages beyond those intended by the author. One example of this conundrum is evident in my decision to assign a descriptor to the students who were the primary focus of this research. I chose to use "Canford" to describe transfer program students and "neighborhood" to describe their Arbor Town school peers. These labels are by no means perfectly precise, although I found them much more appropriate than terms such as "majority" and "minority," which were too vague, imprecise, and loaded to be effective. Additionally, there is much discussion and debate in the literature around the use of terms such as "African American" or "black" in describing American slave descendants (Baugh, 1999). Similarly, the use of expressions such as "participants," "subjects," or "others" to describe individuals who participate in research is also debated (Glesne and Peshkin, 1992). While an extended discussion of the use and meaning of these and other terms is well warranted, I will not endeavor to do so here. Still, I would like to note that I have attempted to be thoughtful in my choice of words, particularly ones I have chosen as labels and descriptors. I remain open to suggestions to better approaches to such thorny issues.

Another complication arose in the rendering of transcripts from interviews and conversations, where one must make decisions about formatting, syntax, and affect in rendering human speech. Such work is quite complicated and much can be gained and lost, both consciously and unconsciously, in the process. For example, written versions of spoken language are often expressed in ways that distinguish the "other" from an unacknowledged "norm." The vernacular of African American speech, for instance, is often painstakingly transcribed in ways that emphasize minor details in usage, while within the same work the speech of whites may be relayed in ways that conform to standard, written English. Clearly, though, such works are inattentive to variations between written and spoken forms of language that occur in all speakers. In this book I have attempted to transcribe materials from all speakers in a common fashion, generally not distinguishing speech forms below the level of the word. For various reasons, I tended to be more concerted in my efforts to distinguish speech patterns among the youth in my study than among adults.[4]

Finally, other decisions I have made in the writing process are perhaps unconventional, though certainly not novel. For example, in this work's narratives I write about the experiences of the Canford students primarily in the present tense to help draw the reader into their lives and their world, though of course the events have long since passed. Also, while from time to time I did use a recorder in my fieldwork, many of the quotations included here are derived from my best attempts to re-create conversations based on handwritten field notes and memory, although I realize that they are imperfect tools. The structure and coherence of the narratives and the work as a whole are another construct of the author's craft. Reality is murky, three-dimensional (at least), and difficult to grasp, much less to render. All writing—and all research—in some sense then is a fiction. One cannot possibly capture reality or the "truth" in this form or any other. The decisions and judgments of the author help to create perhaps a slice of reality or a reflection of it, ideally one that is informative and elucidating for the reader. Clearly my job as a writer and researcher is not to re-create every detail of every event I witnessed but rather to share with the reader the substance of what it is that these children have taught me about their lives. I have worked to do so in a manner and form that are conducive to making a meaningful rendering of these lessons for others. Every choice, of course, has an impact on the product, both purposeful and unintended. My hope is that in sharing some of these decisions with my readers, I allow them to make better judgments for themselves about the work.

Notes

Chapter One:
Beginnings

1. To help protect the confidentiality of participants, I have used pseudonyms for all individuals, schools, school districts, localities, program titles and other entities named in this book. In some cases, distinguishing characteristics of students, teachers, classrooms, or schools have been altered as well to help protect the identities of participants. All of the descriptions, narratives, and quotations related here are based on actual events, observations, interviews, and discussions.

2. See Darling-Hammond (1997) for further discussion about the development of schools and systems that support the learning of all children.

3. I have chosen to use the term "neighborhood" to describe non-Canford students in Arbor Town schools. While an imperfect and imprecise term in some ways, it seems preferable to and more accurate than any other I considered. I also generally refer to students in the Canford Program as either Canford or transfer students. See the appendix for further discussion of issues relating to writing and method.

4. Other scholars have looked from slightly different angles at programs with some similarities to the Canford Program. For example, in *Stepping over the Color Line* (1997), Amy Stuart Wells and Robert Crain provide an exceptional view of the development and implementation of the St. Louis desegregation program, providing a rich historical context for the program and an insightful investigation of the outcomes for program graduates based on extensive interviews combined with survey and data analysis. In *The Other Boston Busing Story* (2001), Susan Eaton explores METCO, a voluntary

transfer program that places children from Boston's city schools into surrounding suburban districts. Eaton relies principally on interviews with program graduates as she explores the benefits and drawbacks of the program.

Chapter Two:
The Canford Program

1. My goal here is not an exhaustive history but rather a contextual backdrop. A reader interested in a more in-depth exploration of the legal, political, and social history of school desegregation will find numerous sources on the topic. For example, in *Dismantling Desegregation: The Quiet Reversal of "Brown v. Board of Education"* (1996) Gary Orfield and Susan Eaton review the legal history of school desegregation while focusing on more recent decisions by the Rehnquist Court as well as social and political trends that seem to undermine prior gains in school desegregation.

2. Orfield and Lee (2005).

3. Joondeph (1999).

4. Source material for this paragraph and the two following paragraphs comes from a Ph.D. dissertation completed in 1989 and a locally published book focusing on the history of the region under discussion (publication information for both sources withheld for reasons of confidentiality).

5. Source material for this passage comes from a book privately printed in 2002 (publication information withheld for reasons of confidentiality).

6. Canford et al. v. Arbor Town School District and the State of California et al. (1976).

7. Canford et al. v. Superior Court (1983).

8. Canford et al. v. Arbor Town School District and the State of California et al. (1986).

9. Center for Educational Planning, County Office of Education (2001). Note that one of the districts is no longer covered by the Canford agreement, as in 1991 it reached a status of more than 60 percent minorities. Thus the current number of available slots in the Canford Program each year is 166 rather than the 206 originally indicated.

10. Center for Educational Planning, County Office of Education (2001).

11. Center for Educational Planning, County Office of Education (2002).

12. Taylor (1998a).

13. Taylor (1998a); Taylor (1998b); Arbor Town School District (1995); personal interviews (2001, 2002).

Chapter Three:
The Bus Kids

1. The kindergarten schedules in Arbor Town vary from school to school. At the time of this study, several kindergarten classrooms alternated between full- and half-day schedules, allowing teachers time to work with a smaller group of students on some afternoons.

2. In the literature on busing there is a paucity of research on the *experience* and the *impact* of riding a school bus, although it is a ubiquitous feature of American schooling. Most of such scholarship is focused on policies and practices related to school desegregation or the financial and bureaucratic considerations inherent in this endeavor. Very little attention is given to the impact of the experience on the lives of children.

3. While I highlight some clearly deleterious effects of bus rides on the Canford students' daily school lives, I do not mean to imply that busing, per se, is either beneficial or detrimental to larger educational or societal aims. Busing is a complicated political and social issue, and I do not attempt a resolution here. At the same time, it is safe to say that alleviating some of the hardships encountered on this journey would surely be of service to participating children.

Chapter Four:
Friends

1. See, for example, Corsaro (1985); Schneider (2000); and Paley (1993).

2. Some of the numerous research studies linking student outcomes with social dynamics include Ladd and Price (1987); Ladd (1990); Birch and Ladd (1996); Wentzel (1991); and Hartup and Stevens (1997).

3. I derived this practice in part from the works of Vivian Gussin Paley, including *The Girl with the Brown Crayon* (1997) and *The Boy Who Would Be a Helicopter* (1990), in which she describes her own practice of using storytelling to better understand the children in her classrooms.

4. Corsaro (1985) described a similar phenomenon that he dubbed "protection of interactive space."

Chapter Six:
Leopards and Chameleons

1. There is a great deal of scholarship on the development of racial identity in children. For just two such examples see Tatum (1997) and Lewis (2004). Interestingly, most scholars in this field focus their attention on early adolescents or teens, perhaps believing that they are more likely either to comprehend or at least to express more clearly their developing under-standings of these complex issues. Discussions in the literature about racial identity in the preschool and primary years focus more on the questions of children's abilities to identify and classify racial categories. See, for example, Aboud and Doyle (1993) and Phinney (1993). The experiences of the Canford students in my study suggest that children as young as five begin to grapple seriously with racial, linguistic, and cultural identity. Perhaps being part of a small minority group within a predominantly white and Asian school popu-lation motivates this early consideration of racial and ethnic identity. More research with these younger populations is warranted in this arena.

2. This text and all other quotations from Spanish-speaking parents are based on the translation of an interpreter present during my interviews with Canford parents.

3. See, for example, Baugh (1999).

Chapter Seven:
The Grown-Ups

1. Parents apply to the Canford Program generally and not to a specific district, although they may rank their top three preferences. Arbor Town is the most sought-after district—nearly all of the Canford parents rate the district as their first choice. This helps to explain why the parents in the fol-lowing discussion compare these two districts in particular rather than weigh the choice between South Bay City and a general transfer. This pattern also underscores the fact that parents may not be fully informed in their de-cision making, as many children whose applications to the Canford Program request placement in Arbor Town are either sent to another district or not accepted at all if spaces are no longer available.

2. A comparison of the two districts on California's Academic Perfor-mance Index in 2000 reveals that twelve of Arbor Town's thirteen elementary and middle schools achieved the highest rating, a 10 out of 10. The other school rated a 9. Of South Bay City's eleven elementary and middle schools,

only two schools ranked above a 3. In the state's "similar schools" ranking, which compares schools with comparable demographics, South Bay City schools fared a bit better. Two of its schools rated a 10 and one other rated an 8, though seven of the schools still ranked 3 or below. In the similar schools ranking, seven of Arbor Town's thirteen schools rated a 9 or a 10. See California Department of Education (2003a).

3. For example, at the time of this study, the district offered each Canford student several hours of tutoring support to be used during the first two years in the program, as a way to help students who might need additional support to "catch up" academically. But several teachers commented that they had difficulty finding and arranging for tutors, and they were provided with little support by the district in doing so. Most Canford parents and several district teachers I spoke with were unaware of this program.

4. See Wells and Crain (1997) and Lewis (2004) for further discussion of the concept of a "color-blind perspective" in the matter of race relations in schools.

Chapter Eight:
Teaching Styles

1. See Jackson (1990) and Lortie (1977) for classic descriptions of teachers at their craft. Many of the elements described in those works pervaded the practices of the teachers in this study as well.

2. Lave and Wenger's (1991) notion of apprenticeship is broader than the traditional organization of craft production and guild relationships that are commonly thought of. As the authors state, "We emphasize the diversity of historical forms, cultural traditions, and modes of production in which apprenticeship is found. . . . [Much] learning occurs in the form of some sort of apprenticeship especially wherever high levels of knowledge and skills are in demand (e.g., medicine, law, the academy, professional sports, and the arts)" (63).

3. See Bourdieu (1977) and Stanton-Salazar (1997), for example.

Chapter Nine:
The Road Ahead

1. See Eaton (2001) for an example.

2. John Baugh (1999) provides a useful discussion relevant to this

point. Baugh critiques a 1985 federal report entitled *What Works: Research about Teaching and Learning,* noting that the stated framework of the report is organized around the ill-defined "typical" or "average" student. What is clearly lacking from the report and perhaps from too many of today's educational policies and practices is an understanding of the varying needs of diverse students across a range of settings. Baugh suggests that the notion of a "homogenized" set of educational practices for a diverse student population is generally ineffective and counterproductive (16).

3. Ferguson (1991); Goldhaber and Brewer (1997); Sanders and Rivers (1996).

4. As mentioned previously, the work of Wells and Crain (1997), Eaton (2001), and Crain (1984) provides thoughtful examples of research that looks at some of the long-term effects of participation in desegregation programs in St. Louis, Boston, and Hartford, respectively.

Appendix

1. Barker's *One Boy's Day* (1951) offers an early example of intensive "shadowing" in the field. For further discussions of artifact-based interviews and other uses of "evocative stimuli" see Spindler and Spindler (1987) and Graue and Walsh (1998).

2. On "subjectivities," see Peshkin (1991).

3. Parents provided the primary consent for student participation in this study. I also note that the Human Subjects Review Board required the signature of the students on consent forms, a decision I was not fully comfortable with myself. I agreed that students should have a choice as to their specific participation in research related activities, and I always provided students with a choice to opt out of any direct research activities such as interviews. At the same time, I felt that it was rather unlikely that the students truly could be fully informed about the nature of the enterprise, and thus their signatures on the consent forms seemed somehow inappropriate. This is one of the many ethical and methodological issues that arose for me in the conduct of this research.

4. Two reasons account for the difference in transcription treatment of children and adults in this work, though such distinctions are still minor and perhaps subtle. First, most of the transcriptions of adults came from semistructured interviews. Moreover, I had assistance from outside sources in transcribing those interviews. In contrast, much of the speech quoted from the children was taken from a more "natural" context, and I transcribed

all utterances from the children myself. Additionally, for narrative and aesthetic purposes, it seemed reasonable to attend more carefully to the tone and flow of the children's speech than to that of the adults. I am indebted to Ray McDermott for his assistance and guidance on this and many other important issues (personal communication, McDermott, 2003).

References

To protect the confidentiality of participants, I have used pseudonyms for all individuals, schools, school districts, localities, program titles, and other entities named in this book. These pseudonyms are retained in citations of court cases, school district publications, and local periodicals.

Aboud, F., & Doyle, A. (1993). The early development of ethnic identity and attitudes. In M. Bernal & G. Knight (Eds.), *Ethnic identity* (47–60). Albany: State University of New York Press.

Anson, R. (1987). *Best intentions: The education and killing of Edmund Perry.* New York: Random House.

Arbor Town School District. (1995). *Canford voluntary transfer program, 1995–96* (A report to the board of education of the Arbor Town School District). Arbor Town, CA: Arbor Town School District.

Arbor Town School District. (2001). *2001–2002 Ethnic report by school.* Arbor Town, CA: Arbor Town School District.

Azri, Y., & Amir, Y. (1977). Intellectual and academic achievements and adjustment of underprivileged children in homogeneous and heterogeneous classrooms. *Child Development* 48: 726–729.

Barker, R. (1951). *One boy's day.* New York: Harper.

Barone, T. (2001). *Touching eternity.* New York: Teachers College Press.

Baugh, J. (1999). *Out of the mouths of slaves.* Austin: University of Texas Press.

Baugh, J. (2000). *Beyond Ebonics.* New York: Oxford University Press.

Becker, H. (1998). *Tricks of the trade.* Chicago: University of Chicago Press.

Becker, H., & Geer, B. (1982). Participant observation: The analysis of qualitative field data. In R. Burgess (Ed.), *Field research: A sourcebook and field manual* (239–250). London: George Allen and Unwin.

Birch, S., & Ladd, G. (1996). Interpersonal relationships in the school environment. In J. Juvonen & K. Wentzel (Eds.), *Social motivation: Understanding children's school adjustment*. New York: Cambridge University Press.

Borland, J., Schnur, R., & Wright, L. (2000). Economically disadvantaged students in a school for the academically gifted: A postpositivist inquiry into individual and family adjustment. *Gifted Child Quarterly* 44: 13–32.

Bourdieu, P. (1977). *Outline of a theory of practice*. Cambridge: Cambridge University Press.

Brizuela, B., & Garcia-Sellers, M. (1999). School adaptation: A triangular process. *American Educational Research Journal* 36: 345–370.

Brown v. Board of Education. 347.S.438 (1954).

California Department of Education. (2003a). *Academic Performance Index* [Online]. http://api.cde.ca.gov/.

California Department of Education. (2003b). *California's reading first program: As approved by the United States Department of Education* [Online]. http://www.cde.ca.gov/board/readingfirst/index.html.

California Department of Education. (2003c). *No Child Left Behind: State of California* [Online]. http://www.cde.ca.gov/pr/nclb/.

Canford et al. v. Arbor Town School District and the State of California et al. (1976). Identifying information suppressed.

Canford et al. v. Arbor Town School District and the State of California et al. (1979). Identifying information suppressed.

Canford et al. v. Superior Court. (1983). Identifying information suppressed.

Canford et al. v. Arbor Town School District and the State of California et al. (1986). Settlement Order. Superior Court of the State of California. Identifying information suppressed.

Center for Educational Planning, County Office of Education. (2001). *Canford Voluntary Transfer Plan: 2000–2001 Compliance Report*. Redwood County, CA: County Office of Education.

Center for Educational Planning, County Office of Education. (2002). *Canford Voluntary Transfer Plan: 2001–2002 Compliance Report*. Redwood County, CA: County Office of Education.

Charmaz, K. (1983). The grounded theory method: An explication and interpretation. In R. Emerson (Ed.), *Contemporary field research* (109–126). Boston: Little, Brown.

Corsaro, W. (1985). *Friendship and peer culture in the early years*. Westport, CT: Ablex Publishing.

Crain, R., Hawes, J., Miller, R., & Peichert, J. (1984). *A longitudinal study of a metropolitan voluntary desegregation plan*. Washington, DC: National Institute of Education.

Darling-Hammond, L. (1997). *The right to learn*. San Francisco: Jossey-Bass.

Davidson, A. (1999). Negotiating social differences: Youths' assessments of educators' strategies. *Urban Education* 34(3): 338–369.

Delpit, L. (1995). *Other people's children*. New York: New Press.

Dewey, J. (1934). *Art as experience*. New York: Perigee Books.

Dewey, J. (1938). *Experience and education*. New York: Simon & Schuster.

Eaton, S. (2001). *The other Boston busing story*. New Haven: Yale University Press.

Eisner, E. (1994). *Cognition and curriculum reconsidered*. New York: Teachers College Press.

Eisner, E. (1997). The promise and perils of alternative forms of data representation. *Educational Researcher* 26(6): 4–11.

Eisner, E. (1998). *The enlightened eye: Qualitative inquiry and the enhancement of educational practice*. Upper Saddle River, NJ: Prentice-Hall.

Eisner, E. (2003). Questionable assumptions about our schools. *Kappan* 84(9): 648–657.

Ferguson, R. F. (1991). Paying for public education: New evidence on how and why money matters. *Harvard Journal on Legislation* 28(2): 465–498.

Fine, G., & Sandstrom, K. (1998). *Knowing children: Participant observation with minors*. Newbury Park, CA: Sage Publications.

Fox, M. (1996). Rural school transportation as a daily constraint in students' lives. *Rural Educator* 17(2): 22–27.

Geertz, C. (1973). *The interpretation of cultures*. New York: Basic Books.

Glesne, C., & Peshkin, A. (1992). *Becoming a qualitative researcher*. New York: Longman.

Goldhaber, D. D., & Brewer, D. J. (1997). Evaluating the effect of teacher degree level on educational performance. In W. J. Fowler (Ed.), *Developments in School Finance, 1996* (197–210). Washington, DC: National Center for Education Statistics, U.S. Department of Education.

Graue, M., & Walsh, D. (1998). *Studying children in context*. Thousand Oaks, CA: Sage Publications.

Green, R. (1966). After school integration—what? Problems in social learning. *Personnel and Guidance Journal* 44: 704–710.

Green v. County School Board. 391 U.S. 430 (1968).

Hartup, W. (1996). The company they keep: Friendships and their developmental significance. *Child Development* 67: 1–13.

Hartup, W., & Stevens, N. (1997). Friendships and adaptation in the life course. *Psychological Bulletin* 121: 355–370.

Holmes, R. (1995). *How young children perceive race*. Thousand Oaks, CA: Sage Publications.

Holmes, R. (1998). *Fieldwork with children*. Thousand Oaks, CA: Sage Publications.

Howley, C., & Smith, C. (2000). *An agenda for studying rural school busing*. Washington, DC: Office of Educational Research and Improvement.

Intrator, S. (1999). Spots of time that glow. Ph.D. diss., Stanford University.

Jackson, P. (1990). *Life in classrooms*. (Revised ed.) New York: Teachers College Press.

Joondeph, B. (1993). Killing Brown softly: The subtle undermining of effective desegregation in *Freeman v. Pitts. Stanford Law Review* 46(1): 147–174.

Joondeph, B. (1998). Skepticism and school desegregation. *Washington University Law Quarterly* 76(1): 161–170.

Joondeph, B. (1999). A second redemption? *Washington and Lee Law Review* 56(1): 169–232.

Ladd, G. (1996). Shifting ecologies during the five to seven year period: Predicting children's adjustment during the transition to grade school. In A. J. Sameroff & M. M. Haith (Eds.), *The five to seven year shift: The age of reason and responsibility* (363–386). Chicago: University of Chicago Press.

Ladd, G. (1990). Having friends, keeping friends, making friends, and being liked by peers in the classroom: predictors of children's early school adjustment? *Child Development* 61: 1081–1100.

Ladd, G., & Price, J. (1987). Predicting children's social and school adjustment following the transition from preschool to kindergarten. *Child Development* 58: 1168–1189.

Lave, J., & Wenger, E. (1991). *Situated learning: Legitimate peripheral participation*. Cambridge: Cambridge University Press.

Lewis, A. (2004). *Race in the schoolyard: Negotiating the color line in classrooms and communities*. New Brunswick, NJ: Rutgers University Press.

Lofland, J. (1974). Styles of reporting qualitative field research. *American Sociologist* 9: 101–111.

Lortie, D. (1977). *Schoolteacher*. Chicago: University of Chicago Press.

McDermott, R. P. (1987). The explanation of minority school failure, again. *Anthropology and Education Quarterly* 18(4): 361–364.

McDermott, R. P. (1993). The acquisition of a child by a learning disability. In S. Chaiklin & J. Lave (Eds.), *Understanding practice* (269–305). Cambridge: Cambridge University Press.

Merton, R. (1987). Three fragments from a sociologist's notebooks: Establishing the phenomenon, specified ignorance, and strategic research materials. *Annual Review of Sociology* 13: 1–28.

Miles, M., & Huberman, A. M. (1984). Drawing valid meaning from qualitative data: Toward a shared craft. *Educational Researcher* 13(5): 20–30.

Nespor, J. (1997). *Tangled up in school: Politics, bodies, and signs in the educational process.* Mahwah, NJ: Lawrence Erlbaum Associates.

Orfield, G., Arenson, J., Jackson, T., Bohrer, C., Gavin, D., & Kalejs, E. (1998). City-suburban desegregation: Parent and student perspectives in metropolitan Boston. *Equity and Excellence in Education* 31: 6–12.

Orfield, G., & Eaton, S. (1996). *Dismantling desegregation: The quiet reversal of "Brown v. Board of Education."* New York: New Press.

Orfield, G., & Lee, C. (2005). New faces, old patterns? Segregation in the multiracial South. A report of the Civil Rights Project, Harvard University.

Paley, V. (1984). *Boys and girls: Superheroes in the doll corner.* Chicago: University of Chicago Press.

Paley, V. (1990). *The boy who would be a helicopter.* Cambridge: Harvard University Press.

Paley, V. (1993). *You can't say you can't play.* Cambridge: Harvard University Press.

Paley, V. (1997). *The girl with the brown crayon: How children use stories to shape their lives.* Cambridge: Harvard University Press.

Paley, V. (2000). *White teacher.* Cambridge: Harvard University Press.

Peshkin, A. (1991). In search of subjectivity—one's own. In A. Peshkin, *The color of strangers, the color of friends* (appendix, 285–295). Chicago: University of Chicago Press.

Peshkin, A. (1993). The goodness of qualitative research. *Educational Researcher* 22(2): 23–29.

Peshkin, A. (1994). *Growing up American: Schooling and the survival of community.* Prospect Heights, IL: Waveland Press.

Peshkin, A. (1997). *Places of memory: Whiteman's schools and Native American communities.* Mahwah, NJ: Lawrence Erlbaum Associates.

Peshkin, A. (2000). The nature of interpretation in qualitative research. *Educational Researcher* 29(9): 5–9.

Phelan, P., Davidson, A., & Cao, H. (1991). Students' multiple worlds: Negotiating the boundaries of family, peer, and school cultures. *Anthropology and Education Quarterly* 22(3): 224–250.

Phelan, P., Davidson, A., & Yu, H. (1998). *Adolescents' words: Negotiating family, peer, and school.* New York: Teachers College Press.

Phinney, J. (1993). A three-stage model of ethnic identity development in adolescence. In M. Bernal & G. Knight (Eds.), *Ethnic identity* (61–80). Albany: State University of New York Press.

Platt, J. (1992). "Cases of cases . . . of cases." In C. Ragin & H. Becker (Eds.), *What is a Case?* (21–52). Cambridge: Cambridge University Press.

Pope, D. (1999). *Doing school.* Ph.D. diss., Stanford University.

Pope, D. (2001). *Doing school.* New Haven: Yale University Press.

Raley, J., Pope, D., Steyer, I., & Lit, I. (2001). What the shadow knows: A close examination of a research method. An interactive symposium presentation given at the annual conference of the American Educational Research Association. Seattle, WA, April.

Rogoff, B. (1995). Observing sociocultural activity on three planes: Participatory appropriation, guided participation, and apprenticeship. In J. Wertsch, P. del Rio, & A. Alvarez (Eds.), *Sociocultural Studies of Mind* (139 – 162). Cambridge: Cambridge University Press.

Ryan, J., & Heise, M. (2002). The political economy of school choice. *Yale Law Journal* 111(8): 2045 – 2136.

Sanders, W. L., & Rivers, J. C. (1996). *Cumulative and residual effects of teachers on future student academic achievement.* Knoxville: University of Tennessee Value-Added Research and Assessment Center.

Schneider, B. (2000). *Friends and enemies: Peer relations in childhood.* New York: Oxford University Press.

Slate, J. (1996). *Miss Bindergarten gets ready for kindergarten.* New York: Dutton Books.

Spence, B. (2000). Long school bus rides: Their effect on school budgets, family life, and student achievement [Online]. *Rural Education Issue Digest.* http://www.ael.org/rel/rural/pdf/digest1.pdf.

Spindler, G. D., & Spindler, L. (1987). *Interpretive ethnography of education: At home and abroad.* New York: Holt, Rinehart, & Winston.

Spradley, J. (1979). *The ethnographic interview.* Fort Worth: Harcourt Brace Jovanovich.

Stanton-Salazar, R. (1997). A social capital framework for understanding the socialization of racial minority children and youths. *Harvard Educational Review* 67(1): 1 – 40.

Swann v. Charlotte-Mecklenburg Board of Education. 402 U.S. 1 (1971).

Tatum, B. (1997). *"Why are all the black kids sitting together in the cafeteria?"* New York: Basic Books.

Taylor, A. (1998a). *Status report of the Canford voluntary transfer desegregation program—part 1.* A Report to the Board of Education of the Arbor Town School District. Arbor Town, CA: Arbor Town School District.

Taylor, A. (1998b). *Status report of the Canford voluntary transfer desegregation program—part 2.* A Report to the Board of Education of the Arbor Town School District. Arbor Town, CA: Arbor Town School District.

Taylor, S., & Bogdan, R. (1998). *Introduction to qualitative research methods.* New York: John Wiley & Sons.

Tharp, R., Estrada, P., Dalton, S., & Yamauchi, L. (2000). *Teaching transformed.* Boulder: Westview Press.

Tharp, R., & Gallimore, R. (1988). *Rousing minds to life.* Cambridge: Cambridge University Press.

United States Department of Education. (2003). *No Child Left Behind* [Online]. http://www.ed.gov/nclb/landing.jhtml.

Varenne, H., & McDermott, R. P. (1998). *Successful failure.* Boulder: Westview Press.

Wells, A., & Crain, R. (1997). *Stepping over the color line.* New Haven: Yale University Press.

Wentzel, K. (1991). Relations between social competence and academic achievement in early adolescence. *Child Development* 62: 1066–1078.

Winter, G. (2003). Schools resegregate, study finds. *New York Times,* January 21.

Zars, B. (1998). Long rides, tough hides: Enduring long school bus rides [Online]. *Rural Challenge Policy Program.* http://www.ruralchallengepolicy.org/zars_busing.htm.

Index